Violence in the Middle East

Violence
in the Middle East

From Political Struggle
to Self-Sacrifice

Hamit Bozarslan

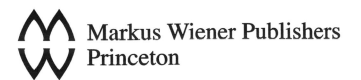

Markus Wiener Publishers
Princeton

For information write to:
Markus Wiener Publishers
231 Nassau Street
Princeton, NJ 08542
www.markuswiener.com

   Library of Congress Cataloging-in-Publication Data

Bozarslan, Hamit.
  Violence in the Middle East : from political struggle to self-sacrifice /
Hamit Bozarslan.
      p. cm.
Includes bibliographical references and index.
  ISBN 1-55876-308-2 (hardcover : alk. paper)
  ISBN 1-55876-309-0 (paperback)
  1. Political violence. 2. Political violence--Middle East.   I. Title.

JC328.6 .B693 2004
303.6'2'0956--dc22
                                                      2003027395

Contents

Preface   vii

Introduction   1

I   Minority Issues and Violence:
From Nationalist Claims to Self-Sacrifice Among the Kurds   19

II From Political Struggle to Self-Sacrifice:
Violence in Turkey   59

III From Instrumental Violence to Self-Sacrifice
in the Middle East   99

Conclusion   139

Appendix   A Brief Comment on Methodology   143

Notes   151

Preface

The present study is the product of a long period of reflection on various issues related to political violence in the Middle East. My sole aim here is to offer a set of hypotheses to shed light on political violence in this region, which only future monographs and comparative studies can confirm or discredit.

I have discussed some of these hypotheses with my colleagues at EHESS[1]—Alain Joxe, Farhad Khosrokavar, Daniel Pecaut, Lucette Valensi, Michel Wieviorka; with Georges Elwert and Pénélope Larzillère, fellow participants on a panel on violence organized by IISMM[2] in Paris; and with the participants in my seminar on the history and sociology of violence in the Middle East at EHESS. Conversations with Martin van Bruinessen, Jean Leca, Rémy Leveau, Şerif Mardin, Elizabeth Picard, and Semih Vaner also contributed to the development of the hypotheses presented herein.

The invitation by the Program in Near Eastern Studies to deliver the 2002 Poullada Lectures at Princeton University allowed me to present my hypotheses to a larger audience, and the careful editing of Michael Reynolds, Kristin Gilbert, and Susan Lorand helped transform the lectures into this book.

I thank all of the above mentioned for their invaluable contributions and assistance. I alone am responsible for any and all flaws that remain.

Introduction

By the end of the 1990s, in spite of the region's chronic instability, the societies of the Middle East appeared to be drawing closer to achieving domestic peace. The radical Islamist movement was giving signs of weakening in all the countries of the Middle East. In Algeria, violence[3] was limited to the "Algérie inutile" (part of Algeria whose protection is not of strategic importance) and a state of calm held in the major cities. In Egypt, the operations of the Gama'a Islamiyya were confined to the Upper Nile region. In Turkey, the guerrilla warfare of the PKK was waning, and the violent acts of both radical leftist and Islamist groups were at most sporadic. In Palestine/Israel a seemingly fruitful cooperation between the Israeli and Palestinian authorities "regulated" and limited violence to a significant extent. The general expectation was that the outgoing Clinton administration would broker a viable peace agreement that would lead to a reasonably peaceful coexistence between Israelis and Palestinians.

Then came the suicide attacks of the second Intifada and those of September 11, 2001. These attacks put violence in the Middle East back on the world's agenda. The September 11 attacks petrified millions of viewers of television across the world not just with the high number of victims they claimed so abruptly, but also with their incredible visual impact. They possessed an apocalyptic scale. They defied

1

comparison with any repertoire of violence with which either average citizens or even researchers were familiar. They were not the most deadly attacks in the history of violence, but they were among the most instantaneous ones. As at Hiroshima, Nagasaki, and Halabdja, time itself had seemingly been obliterated during the attacks of September 11. The beginning and the end were collapsed into one. Unlike what occurred in the three other cases cited above, however, in the attacks of September 11 nineteen hijackers collectively transformed their bodies into weapons. The destruction of their own bodies was the necessary condition for the violence they directed at others.

Although the collective aspect of this self-sacrifice struck many observers, the self-sacrifice itself was not a new phenomenon. Long before September 11, in at least three countries—Sri Lanka, Kurdistan/Turkey, and Israel/Palestine—human bodies were used as integral parts of explosive munitions. With this new weapon system, violence itself changed form and meaning in these regions.

Violence, Anomie and Terrorism

Social scientists failed to understand this transformation, to notice that something new was happening in Palestine and in Turkey, or even to perceive that an old *technique* of violence used during the Second World War by Japanese kamikazes was being resurrected in different parts of the world. Fear, as well as ideological and normative blinders, was partly accountable for this incapacity. One often forgets that social scientists are also citizens, and it is understandable that, like other citizens, they too are often more eager to condemn and then look beyond this enigmatic phenomenon rather than to probe and explain it.

But this incapacity was also at least partly linked to the professional rather than personal reluctance of social scientists to address and analyze the issues surrounding violence. As late as 1968 Hannah Arendt noted that the social sciences lacked adequate concepts and instruments for understanding and explicating violence.[4] Since 1968 more research has been done on the issue of violence, but to a large extent violence still remains a sort of "taboo" topic. I will give just two examples. The famous *Dictionnaire de la sociology* of the *Encylopaedia Universalis*, whose preparation required the mobilization of nearly all well-known French sociologists, all but ignores the question of violence. Violence as a topic appears only twice, and as a part of two other entries: "délinquence" (small-time criminality) and "television."[5] Similarly, the standard reference work of French sociology, the *Dictionnaire de Sociologie*, devotes less than half of a page to the topic of "collective violence."[6]

Many reasons might explain this reluctance. Throughout their history, the social sciences, and in particular sociology, strove to recognize and define regular patterns and, ultimately, to use knowledge of these patterns to predict future social behavior. Violence, however, is a profoundly destructive phenomenon. The reality of violence reveals that the frontiers between the fundamental categories of social sciences—individual, private, and public spheres—can be totally destroyed; and that people can prefer death, regression, or destruction to life, progress, and material wealth. Simultaneously, violence also testifies to the fragility of a social contract or of the legitimacy of a given political order, and so undermines political certainties as well as personal ones.

Thus violence too often has been linked to "anomie"—the exact antithesis of social regulation and rational social behavior—or analyzed as "terrorism." Both concepts fail, however, to fully explain the complexity of violence. Anomie, or its multiple synonyms so often invoked since September 11, means, ultimately, an incapacity to elaborate a rational interpretation of the world, if not a complete radical cognitive deregulation. But certainly in some cases violence can be explained by very rational choices, or at least by a combination of rational calculations and subjective perceptions of social relations. The fact that perpetrators of violence often fail does not mean that their violence is not rational or not instrumental. Moreover, a violence that destroys material wealth and human lives might be employed by rational political actors to enable a given power to sustain itself or to change the existing power relations to their advantage. The destruction of wealth might be an economic disaster for a society in its *totality*, but it may be politically, or even economically, rational for the *particular* actors using violence. Even some self-sacrificial forms of violence can ultimately be linked to a rational calculation. A person's self-destruction cannot be explained by his or her own individual benefits, but it can bring rational, material, or symbolic resources to a political and/or military *organization*. Thus it cannot be said that all violence is based on a disregard for reason.

Nor can we lump all violence into the box labeled "terrorism." As a concept, terrorism is highly normative and, as such, it is of very poor analytical utility for the social sciences. In its broader meaning, terrorism refers to the use of violence by an organization to compel society to accept what it otherwise would have refused. The invocation of the term "terrorism" might allow us to express indignation or to reinforce our normative and ethical positions, but it does not help us understand the aims, motives, and minds of the people who have embraced violence. Moreover, all wars involve the legitimization of constraint and

4

the suppression or destruction of the individual and collective wills of others. All political systems, even democratic ones, involve the legal constraint of persons and parties. At their best, they attempt to balance constraint and freedom, but they do not abandon their need or right to compel.

Models and Paradigms from the 1970s through the 1990s

The social sciences offer some analytical tools that allow us to discuss the phenomenon of violence (but not necessarily the self-sacrificial forms of violence) beyond these simplistic explanations. During the 1970s and 1980s, the emergence of political—and non-political—violence in many societies, including Western ones, in fact obliged social scientists to overcome to some extent their traditional reluctance and pay greater attention to the issue of violence. A few paradigms that tried to overcome the analytical vacuum identified by Hannah Arendt emerged during these decades. These paradigms explained violence either by rational choices or by the concept of "relative deprivation." In a series of works, Charles Tilly has suggested that violence aims at the construction of new power relations, if not at power itself,[7] and posited that the construction of a state is itself the outcome of the rationalized use of violence. Ted Gurr, on the other hand, proposed that violence was a product of relative deprivation. In his model, individuals or social groups perceive a given situation as preventing them from accessing the resources to which they believe they are entitled,[8] and initiate violence in response. More recently, Michel Wieviorka, in his work on violence in France, has offered a new explanation. According to him, violence emerges when conflicts are criminalized, or when the protagonists involved in these conflicts are unable to negotiate the legitimacy of their conflicts. Violence thus ceases to be a consequence of conflicts. Rather, it is understood as the consequence of the denial of conflicts.[9] Wieviorka, like Georges Simmel[10] decades ago, tried to rehabilitate the status of conflict as a decisive element of social cohesion, seeing straightforward conflict as preferable to inchoate violence.

Undoubtedly, these mainstream models continue to explain many cases of violence in the world. In many situations the decision to use violence is taken by a collective rather than a personal actor with its own large-scale calculation of the costs and benefits; in others, the emotions of frustration and anger can push individuals and collective groups to violent forms of action and expression. In almost all cases the criminalization of differences and conflicts plays a role in the passage to violence. Social, political, ethnic, and sectarian groups whose existence or dignity are denied and who do not have access to a legal framework in which they can act often use violence with the goal of improving their conditions.

Nonetheless, while they remain of great use in understanding most situations, these mainstream paradigms do not explain the peculiarly sacrificial forms of violence that we are now observing in some parts of the world. The authors of September 11, for instance, did not aim at any kind of accumulation of power; at most, such a rational objective belonged perhaps to the organization that commanded their destruction, but it could not belong to them personally. They were not, individually at least, victims of relative deprivation. To the contrary, they had more opportunities than did most young Middle Easterners, or even many young Europeans and Americans. They might have been "angry," but their violence was directed as much at the destruction of themselves as it was at the destruction of thousands of victims personally unknown to them. The conflict in which they were protagonists was not criminalized; they certainly had the possibility to speak out, to organize themselves into a legitimate political force and conduct a peaceful action, if not in the Middle East itself, then in their host countries of Great Britain, Germany, and the United States. Therefore, the current paradigms, which explain self-sacrificial forms of violence in terms of either rational strategies or frustration, are of poor analytical use. New interdisciplinary approaches, attentive both to long-term structural factors and to socio-cognitive discontinuities, are required. The following pages formulate some hypotheses that take into account these factors and discontinuities.

Rational Violence, Privatized Violence, Self-Sacrificial Violence

Violence has been one of the central political issues of many Middle Eastern countries during the last two decades, either episodically (Syria, Iran), or continually throughout these two decades (Turkey, Egypt, Algeria, Iraq, Afghanistan, and Israel/Palestine). In the following chapters I will try to shed some light on the dynamics of this phenomenon.

All three chapters have a common hypothesis: economy, religion, and culture, which are often presented as the prime factors leading to violence, play only a marginal role in the emergence and centrality of violence in Middle Eastern societies. In fact, except for some sporadic riots, as in Morocco and Egypt, economic conditions in the

Middle East have seldom produced violence. Religion, insofar as it reinforces a set of ultimate, non-negotiable references, does sometimes legitimize violence. But in Muslim societies as in non-Muslim ones, the use of religious references is intimately dependent on power relations. Religion can become a part of the syntax of a violent opposition movement, but it is also a structuring element of the "syntax of domination"[11] of the Middle Eastern states. Depending on the configurations in which it is used, it can legitimize violence against the state or strengthen the state's coercion. Finally, in Middle Eastern societies as elsewhere,[12] culture can always be blamed as a system "banalizing" violence. But Middle Eastern cultural systems, like all cultural systems, also possess significant elements that condemn and can at least regulate violence. For example, as Patrick Haenni has shown, the Egyptian "culture of disturbance," while permitting and even encouraging a diffused violence, can also function as a factor limiting outright political violence.[13] The Islamist movements themselves can play such a role. Some of them, at least in Turkey, Egypt, and Morocco, have been able to elaborate mechanisms of social control which efficiently hinder the resort to violence. I will argue in the following hypotheses that, if economy, religion, and culture do only marginally explain the resort to violence, the power relations and subjective perceptions that the authors of violence have of a given situation are heavily accountable for it.

The first hypothesis underlying the following chapters is that violence in the Middle East is a result primarily of political structures, i.e. the nature of the states and their power relations. The participants in mainstream violent movements aim to change the power relations they contest. Violence, at least during the initial stages, seems to be a quite rational instrument. The second hypothesis is that although these movements weaken as organized efforts in their later stages, they very often give birth to fragmented and privatized forms of violence. The final hypothesis is that, in some situations at least, the decline of the collective movements leads not only to the privatization of violence, but also to its metamorphosis into nihilistic, sacrificial, and/or messianic forms.

A political sociology of violence can easily accept that violence is clearly linked to unequal power relations manifested in material and symbolic domination. Symbolic domination denies the dignity of social, political, ethnic, and sectarian groups by labeling them as atavistic, backward, or subhuman. Dominated groups have understandably regarded this symbolic domination as even less tolerable than economic inequality or exploitation. Although throughout history material conditions have provoked many episodes of violence, both sporadic and organized, in the late twentieth century there has been a strong link between a political/social/religious community's subjective perceptions of a given situation, and violence. Likewise, the groups whose peculiar symbols (e.g. national or sectarian ones for minorities, political ones for dissident groups) were criminalized have often been tempted to defend and legitimize these symbols violently.

Violence has usually aimed at the legitimization and integration of social and political opposition groups or ethnic groups and their symbols. In almost all the instances of which I am aware, violence declined after the widespread recognition of this link between violence and the legitimization and integration of the social, political, and ethnic opposition movements involved. This recognition itself often led to a process of democratization or was a constitutive part of it. Democratization in turn allowed the contesting groups and actors to *desacralize* and re-define their hard-core symbols and claims. The over-all democratic framework also led to the marginalization of actors who persisted in the use of violence, as in the case of the Basque. Violence in the Basque country did not disappear entirely, but it lost the legitimacy it had formerly possessed among the Basques under the Franco regime.

Mainstream violent movements in the Middle East can be linked to the political oppositions that face authoritarian states and power relations, or to marginalized social groups or ethnic and sectarian minorities whose existence has been denied or whose symbolic resources have been forbidden. These political, social, ethnic, and sectarian minorities have often been criminalized or have been considered as real or potential internal enemies. The political structures of these countries have proven chronically incapable of resolving the conflicts related to these multiple identities and affiliations. In some cases, as in Iraq, the nature of the states left no room between violence and total submission to state coercion. In other cases, as in Turkey or Egypt for instance, the subjective perceptions that the political oppositions or ethnic groups held of a given historical situation contributed substantively to the aggrieved party's move from peaceful means of action to violent ones. Either a given situation had been perceived as unacceptable and unchangeable without violence, or the actors who adopted violent strategies misperceived their own capacity to change established power relations. The contesting collective actors sought either to realize their integration in the political systems or to bring down a given political order.

My second hypothesis can be summarized as follows. When a repressive regime does not switch from a coercive authoritarian structure to a democratic one, the violence that opposes it may lead to the overthrow of the regime. But the new regime that comes to power may well be as coercive and authoritarian as the previous one. When violent struggle does not succeed in removing the regimes altogether—as has been the case in the Middle East with the major exception of Iran—the violence, fueled by despair, declines or degenerates into something else.

During recent decades, in fact, in regions of conflict throughout the world the "time factor"—both the passage of time (the aging of generations; gaps between old and new generations) and the perception of one's own time experience—has played a decisive role in the transformation of collective violent struggles. At first it seems that, despite organized opposition, many regimes succeed in demonstrating their viability and even co-opt figures from the violent opposition. The remaining aging generations in the struggles prove to be incapable of both maintaining among themselves the high level of mobilization that violent confrontation demands and recruiting sufficient numbers of partisans from the younger generations, and the coordinated opposition falters or ends altogether.

But the weakening of the collective, organized movements behind the violence does not mean the end of violence. On the contrary, violence continues and reproduces itself over years or even over decades. In some situations it becomes more and more detached from any ideological/political commitment or program and is simply privatized.[14] As the many cases studies presented by François Jean and Christophe Ruffin, Jean Hannoyer, and Georg Elwert attest,[15] violence gives birth to private enterprises and reproduces itself by way of the resources provided by this entrepreneurial transformation. This privatization that we observe in many Middle Eastern areas of conflict (Lebanon, Kurdistan, Afghanistan, Egypt, Algeria) is linked to a simultaneous professionalization of violence that is manifested both in the prestige of being a fighter or warlords and in the proliferation of outward symbols, such as ranks and uniforms. The professionalization of violence did not mean the end of structured political discourses: on the contrary, the "fighters" recognized as heroic figures, both by the outsiders and by their own superiors, were expected to learn and propagate a rigid political syntax. In many cases, the symbols of the contest—the sacralization of martyrs; ideas of a "Golden Age" and a "Glorious Future"—have been kept alive. But those symbols ceased to be mobilizing ones and failed to enlarge the initial circles of militants by recruitment of new fighters. Even in the case of aging Islamist armed groups, they have more in common with the symbols of the decaying East Bloc countries in the late 1980s or with the revolutionary symbols in present-day Iran than with those of the emotionally turbulent beginnings of a violent struggle.

My third and final hypothesis is that in some situations the decline of organized violence not only produces the privatization of violence, but can also lead to the emergence of nihilistic/sacrificial[16] or messianic forms of violence. These kinds of violence, while differing in their outward manifestation, are nonetheless complementary. As Albert Camus suggested half a century ago,[17] there is a direct link between nihilism and self-sacrifice. In both cases individuals might seek to preserve the purity of their own engagement, body and mind, by using violence. In both cases the subjects, in the sociological sense of the word, are unable to become positive subjects, i.e., able to give a positive sense to their own past and to project themselves into a constructive future in an interaction with other human beings. They cannot envisage the realization of their aims in a constructive process that would necessarily involve some degree of compromise; their own destruction thus becomes the very condition of emergence as subjects.

In the case of messianism, the individual actually ceases to be a subject. He or she is transformed into an *actent,* or a simple submissive subject, who executes an eschatological form of violence that God demands as the condition of the peace He promised.

Nihilistic or sacrificial violence and messianic violence can be seen as the products of an unbearable tension: between sacredness on the one hand and rationality or pragmatism on the other. In almost all cases, during the initial, emotional stage of violence, the core constellation of symbolic resources—"the leader," "the party," "the fatherland," "religion," etc.—are entirely sacralized and transformed into non-negotiable structures or blocks. This sacralization is the *sine qua non* condition of an increasing mobilization and the readiness to die. One cannot consent to suppress oneself without being convinced that one's cause (a political leader, a national goal . . .) is the only objective worth living for, and therefore, dying for. Notwithstanding this sacralization, however, in a second stage the mainstream actors of a given opposition movement (Kurdish nationalist, left-opposition, Islamist, etc.) have to move from violence to more and more rational and pragmatic choices in order to achieve measurable political goals.

This move requires that previously sacralized claims be negotiated and, if necessary, abandoned. For example, the PKK, the foremost Kurdish oppositionist actor in Turkey, had to abandon its claim to an independent and unified Kurdistan and accept administrative autonomy, or gradually, even the simple recognition of the cultural rights for Kurds. Mainstream Palestinian actors similarly have had to relinquish the goal of the destruction of Israel and accept the recognition of its 1948 borders in order to negotiate with the international community. Such radical but unavoidable moves cannot be made without compromising with the existing political/social "order," i.e. without corrupting to some degree the purity of the initial maximal program. The failure of a violent political-ideological movement can also compel the actors to swallow their ambitions and switch their goal to integrating themselves as legal actors within the existing political system. In this case, too, they must to acquiesce to the corruption of their initial program. There is, for example, a qualitative gap between the goal of establishing an Islamic Emirate of Egypt and that of attaining recognition as a legal component of the political space of the existing Arab Republic of Egypt.

This move from violence to pragmatism can be an extremely difficult one, especially if the state, i.e., the dominant actor, itself rejects any notion of compromise. In the Kurdish case in Turkey, for instance, the leading Kurdish opposition group's movement towards pragmatism did not bring about any reciprocal response from the state, such as the symbolic recognition of Kurdish identity. Similarly, Israel's merely symbolic acknowledgement of the Palestinians' right to a separate state failed to meet the expectations of a great many Palestinians. In many cases, in spite of the challengers' dramatic switch to pragmatism, the material and/or symbolic domination of the existing power structures (denial of Kurdishness; continuity of Israeli settlements, checkpoints, etc.) persists exactly as it did before. The compromise thus is unilateral and is accordingly perceived by many rank-and-file militants and more numerous non-militant sympathizers as pure capitulation or even betrayal.

In some other cases, there exists an unbearable tension between the rationality and pragmatism of the leading actors (or the inevitable consequences of their military failure) on the one hand, and the holiness of the movement's symbols and principles on the other. The second, the sacrality of the symbols, transforms the first, the pragmatism, into something unacceptable.[18] In both cases, nihilistic/self-sacrificial forms of violence emerge either as a way of attesting to one's own integrity in a world where even the leaders of the struggle are corrupted, or as the sole remaining way to overcome the tension between compromise and sacralization. When legitimized by a religious *da'wa* (appeal), these forms of violence can also lead to messianism, i.e., to the expectation of a peace promised by God, but a peace requiring a preliminary massive violence.

From Political Struggle to Self-Sacrifice: Violence in the Middle East

My intention in this book is to show how throughout the twentieth century, and especially during the last three decades, violence in the Middle East emerged as the product of power relations, authoritarian structures and an absence of integrative social contracts. The criminalization of political, ethnic and sectarian identities and the divisions resulting therefrom have contributed to the formation of a "tragic mind" that perceives violence as the surest provider of justice and hope.

But violent opposition movements in the Middle East failed for two important reasons. First, they were unable to create new patterns of politics. In their praxes they came to resemble the states they fought. They demanded of the societies or groups they claimed to represent the acceptance of alternative unanimisms that were nearly as rigid as the official unanimisms of the states they combated. The societies or would-be social-bases of these actors did not follow them, partly because they would not pay the price they were asked to pay, but also partly because they would not accept these alternative unanimisms.

Second, these movements underestimated the strength of the states they opposed. They had imagined the states as weak and corrupted organs that would topple when pushed. The states, however, proved to be more than formal institutional organs. They turned out to consist of sophisticated webs of power relations that could not only mobilize coercive means, but also lithely play games of patron-client relations and resource-allocating mechanisms. If the states did not win enhanced legitimacy, they managed nonetheless to gain a more and more efficient coercive technicality and to ensure their own durability.

Violence thus declined as a mass phenomenon, but it did not disappear. To the contrary, it adopted either a privatized, nihilistic/ sacrificial, or even messianic form. The emergence of warlords within the PKK and of the so-called *uniformed gangs* in Turkey illustrates the switch to the privatized forms of violence. The suicide attacks by the Kurds of Turkey and by Palestinians, the instances of self-immolation and death-fasts in Turkey, as well as the attacks of September 11 all combined, to different degrees, nihilist/sacrificial and messianic forms of violence.

Understanding these forms of violence requires more than a simple analysis of the conditions in which they emerged. Obviously, they cannot be understood without taking these conditions into account, but they also are not reducible simply to them. To return to September 11 as an example, the attacks took place in a given political climate and radically changed that climate. No doubt the sense many Middle Easterners attached to September 11 was rooted in their perception of this political climate and of the issues of Palestine and Iraq. Following such French political scientists as Olivier Roy and Gilles Kepel,[19] I too submit that the attacks on the United States in fact reflect the declining political fortunes of Islamism as a mass-movement, especially in Egypt and Algeria. It is obvious that many Islamists (and non-Islamists) desired apocalyptic revenge on the regimes qualified as *taghuti* and or on their American "Patron." But many months after the attacks, I am still not sure that the leaders of al-Qaida, or even the hijackers, were motivated in their actions *solely* by the political climate in the region. The main arguments put forward in support of this view, such as the irritation caused by the presence of American forces in the "holy land" of Islam or by American policies on Iraq and Palestine, echo weakly in the documents left behind by the hijackers and even in the first video-taped interview of Bin Laden. In fact, those documents were filled with obscure instructions and affirmations that had nothing to do with either politics or geopolitics. Anyone with even a middling knowledge of Islam could easily understand that these instructions were in absolute opposition to well-established Islamic rituals.[20] Obviously only in-depth research that combines the cognitive, social, and religious sciences, as well as different *problematique*s such as the emergence of a new religiosity, can allow us to understand the logic behind not only those attacks, but also behind the self-sacrificial forms of violence that made these attacks possible. This volume, I hope, will start this process of research.

The three chapters that follow can be read as inquiries in historical sociology. The first one deals with the Kurdish question, and it tries to elucidate the links between minority issues and violence. The second examines Turkey, and aims to identify the conditions for the emergence of violence and to describe the processes of social and communal fragmentation and their impact on violence in this country. The third one is on the Middle East broadly speaking, and attempts to analyze the role of power relations in the emergence and transformation of violence.

All three chapters follow a similar layout. They first approach the issue of violence as a historical phenomenon, conceiving of it as a consequence of the destruction of the classical mechanisms of domination and arbitration, which limited, or at least regulated, the use of violence. Second, they suggest that the nature of the states and their internal power relations—as well as the perceptions that political, social, ethnic, and sectarian groups had of their own positions and of their capability to change those positions—led to violence. My intention is to show that the employment of violence had been, at least during its first stage, rational and instrumental. Finally, I explore the metamorphosis of this rational and instrumental violence during the 1990s. I argue that structured mass violence weakened during this decade, but was replaced either by privatized forms of violence or by nihilistic/self-sacrificial behaviors.

The appendix presents the model used to elaborate this socio-historical theoretical framework.

One last point should be made. In so variegated a region as the Middle East, the horizon in which predictability is possible is a narrow one. Therefore, my analysis attempts to illuminate the phenomenon of violence within its constantly changing context rather than make predictions for the future. It reflects the situation as it was in the first years of the twenty-first century. It is self-evident that both the "domestic" dynamics of each individual Middle Eastern country and the regional dynamics can produce configurations marked by new forms of waves of violence or individualized, self-sacrificial forms of violence—or perhaps even nonviolent forms of expression and action.

CHAPTER ONE

Minority Issues and Violence

From Nationalist Claims to Self-Sacrifice Among the Kurds

An observer who compared the situation in the Kurdish regions of the Middle East after the last Gulf War to that of the 1990s would probably be surprised to find that within a single decade a general process of pacification had supplanted the general state of violence and rebellion. In Iraq, the status quo between Baghdad and the regions under the control of the Iraqi Kurdish organizations that followed the Second Gulf War still held. Although fighting between some Kurdish Islamist factions, mainly *Jund al-Islam* (Soldiers of Islam), a group close to al-Qaida, and other Kurdish organizations, continued sporadically in 2002, the Washington Agreement of 1998, which ended the war between the two major Kurdish factions, remained in force to create the conditions for a new "Kurdish spring." In Iran, although no major juridical or administrative change had taken place since Muhammad Khatami's election as president, nonetheless, civil, political, and cultural resistance largely (albeit not totally) replaced guerrilla warfare as the Kurds' preferred form of resistance against the central government. And, finally, in Turkey, the PKK (Workers' Party of Kurdistan), the defining actor of the Kurdish political space, decided to halt its war and change its program and its name. Only small groups of PKK militants rejected these decisions of their leader, Abdullah

Öcalan. Clashes between PKK fighters and the Turkish security forces became sporadic.

In the Kurdish case, as in many other cases in the Middle East, "pacification" today does not necessarily guarantee a peaceful future. Unresolved issues remain volatile, and the Kurdish issue remains potentially explosive. Only future developments will tell us whether the current peace situation is a passing one or not. Still, after decades of violence, this relatively peaceful moment seems a propitious one for analyzing the history of the Kurdish issue and the violence that has surrounded it for years.

The Kurdish Contest in the Middle East: A Brief Recapitulation

Except for the region's inter-state wars, the Kurdish conflict has been the most deadly conflict in the Middle East since the 1920s. Between 1919 and 1946, dozens of Kurdish rebellions took place in Turkey, Iraq and Iran. The "period of silence," i.e. of non-rebellion, which started at the end of 1946 with the destruction of the autonomous Kurdish Republic in Iran (established that same year), lasted only 15 years. In 1961, Mustafa Barzani, a well-known Kurdish nationalist figure, started a new rebellion in Iraq. Except for the brief period of cease-fire with Baghdad between 1971 and 1974, Barzani's uprising continued until his defeat in 1975. But a new insurgency started later the same year and continued until 1991. In Iran in 1979, in the wake of the fall of the Shah and the Islamic revolution, the Kurdish nationalist organizations took control of the main Kurdish cities. The central government's counter-attacks drove the armed Kurds out of the urban centers, but the Kurds responded with a guerrilla struggle. The guerrilla struggle remained active until the mid-1990s (it continues, but at a much lower intensity, as of this writing). In Turkey, the PKK initiated a guerrilla war in 1984 and continued to wage it until 2000. Since 1961, the number of victims of this conflict in the three countries is estimated to be more than 250,000. According to Human Rights Watch, the Anfal operation alone, conducted by the Iraqi army in 1988–89, produced more than 180,000 victims among the civilian population.[21]

The Kurdish struggle during these decades was essentially structured and military. The Kurdish movements possessed more or less hierarchically organized party structures and armies. The violence they perpetrated was rational/instrumental, in the sense that it sought to change the political and juridical status of the Kurdish minority by winning either independence or some degree of political autonomy. In most cases violence was a reply to the authoritarianism of the states and their refusal to acknowledge the Kurdishness that the majority of the Kurds asserted to be their ethnic and cultural identity. Throughout these decades, the Kurdish movements, including by far the most radical one, the PKK, expressed their willingness to negotiate with the central states and offered to renounce violence in exchange for the recognition of their minimal claims.[22]

But during the 1990s the Kurdish struggle in Turkey gave rise to self-sacrificial forms of violence. In the beginning of that decade, five female PKK sympathizers conducted suicide attacks against military targets. Before the end of the decade, more suicide attacks took place and self-immolation by fire of Kurdish militants become a common form of protest in Turkey and among the Kurds in Europe. Self-sacrificial violence on a massive scale marked the period preceding and following the arrest of the PKK's leader Abdullah Öcalan in Kenya in February 1999. Between November 18, 1998 and July 6, 1999 in Turkey, eight people killed themselves in suicide attacks that took the lives of four other people and injured dozens more. Between October 9, 1998 and June 29, 1999, sixty-four Kurds between the ages of seventeen and sixty-three tried to immolate themselves in Turkey and in Europe. Twenty of them died, and most of the others were seriously injured.[23] The PKK could not condemn the militants and sympathizers who sacrificed their lives for its cause, but at the same time it was engaged in an effort to stop them. Only Öcalan's decision in captivity to abandon the armed struggle at the beginning of 2000 put an end to these acts.[24] Obviously, these forms of violence were quite new in the Kurdish movement. Still, they can also be read as the outcomes of the century-long history of the Kurdish conflict.

The Nineteenth Century:
The First Era of Violence in Kurdistan

Violence in the nineteenth century emerged in the Kurdish regions of both Iran and the Ottoman Empire as a result of the destruction of the classical imperial "tacit contract"[25] and the complex webs of power relations that were part of it. The tacit imperial contract from the beginning of the sixteenth century had accorded in some places a de jure, in some others a de facto autonomy to the Kurdish emirates. Each one of these emirates controlled a Kurdish-inhabited zone. But in the course of the nineteenth century both empires decided as part of their programs of centralization and modernization to eliminate the secondary administrative entities on their land, including the Kurdish emirates.

The destruction of the emirates not only provoked a series of up-risings that continued from 1808 to 1880, but also led to two further consequences that neither Constantinople nor Teheran could foresee. The first was that the tribal structures and dynamics, which had lain dormant under state-like emirates, were reactivated and rejuvenated.[26] The destruction of the emirates had created a political vacuum that the central states could not fill. Moreover, the presence of tens of thousands of poorly equipped and ill-paid soldiers in the Kurdish areas worsened, rather than resolved, the security problems of individuals and collective entities alike. The tribes were the only institutions that could both fill this political vacuum and provide protection to their members and clients. Each Kurdish tribe thus became a *de facto* political and military entity. According to the French traveler Ubicini, who visited the Ottoman Empire in 1848–49, at least one thousand tribal entities emerged in the Kurdish areas to replace the previously existing two dozen or so autonomous emirates.[27]

The second consequence of the destruction of the emirates was that the communal relations that until then had been managed by a series of local mechanisms of subordination and domination became violent. The Armenian community in particular became a target of the now uncontrolled Kurdish tribes. Under the influence of Western nationalist and socialist thoughts, the idea of emancipation and national liberation emerged among the Armenian youth and intelligentsia, giving birth to the first nationalist organizations in this part of the Ottoman Empire. The Armenian nationalism itself in turn helped provoke the emergence of Kurdish nationalism. The spread of a more or less aggressive Turkish nationalism among the Young Turk circles in exile at the turn of the twentieth century also reinforced nationalist feelings among the Kurds. By the end of the century, a cultural, if not precisely political, nationalism was quite well diffused among the Kurdish educated elite.

These two consequences produced, at least in the Ottoman Empire, a third and paradoxical consequence: the integration of some tribes into the state's coercive system. In 1891, Constantinople began enrolling Kurdish tribes into the so-called Hamidiye Light Cavalry Regiments. The formation of these regiments was a result of a new doctrine. As David Kushner has suggested,[28] already during the reign of Sultan Abdul Hamid (1876–1909), the idea of Anatolia as the ultimate sanctuary of the Turks had emerged among the Ottoman bureaucratic elite. And Anatolia, this imagined geographic core of a new Turkishness, had to be reinforced by a Pan-Islamic doctrine that aimed at the tighter integration of the Muslim periphery of the Ottoman Empire. The Kurds, particularly the Hamidiyye Cavalries, were thus considered the principal Muslim elements of a peripheral barrier against the Russian Empire in the South and South-East Anatolia.

The formation of the Hamidiyye Regiments created other advantages for the central Ottoman state. First of all, the Sunni tribes that were integrated into the cavalries naturally benefited from the economic and military resources the center allotted them. This selective allocation of resources produced repeated conflicts between the integrated and the non-integrated tribes, thereby transforming the earlier tribal violence against the state into intra-Kurdish violence. The effect of this rechanneling of hostilities was so great that the tribal violence was, from the standpoint of the center, neutralized to a significant degree. Secondly, the Palace obtained a force for protecting its borders against the Russian Empire and thus another threat was largely removed. Last but not least, the Kurdish tribal dynamics were also canalized against the Armenians. Some of the tribes participated heavily in the Armenian massacres of 1894–96, thereby contributing to the Islamization of this border region. In spite of a series of Kurdish rebellions against the Union and Progress government between 1908 and 1914, the alliance of the regiments with the center continued until the end of the First World War I. The regiments, renamed "Tribal Cavalry Brigades" after 1908, participated heavily in the Armenian genocide of 1915–16. Fearful of Armenian revenge, the Kurds also widely supported the Turkish War of Independence (1919–22).

1920s–1940s: The Second Age of Violence in Kurdistan

The Ottoman defeat in the First World War, however, changed the territorial framework of Kurdishness. The integration of southern Kurdistan into an Iraqi state provoked strong reactions, leading to the first Kurdish rebellions against Baghdad. Although the Kurds in Turkey supported the Kemalist resistance during the War of Independence, this alliance with the Kemalist forces proved to be only an interlude. Later, Kurds rose up in defiance of the newly established and militantly nationalist Republic of Turkey. In Iran also, Kurdish unrest led to an uprising.

Between 1919 and 1925, the Kurdish-state relations worsened simultaneously in Iraq, in Turkey, and in Iran for at least three reasons. The first reason was the division of Ottoman Kurdistan between Turkey, Iraq, and Syria and the militarization of the borders that separated these new entities. This new division of Kurdistan was in fact much more problematic than the first one that resulted from the Qasr-i Chirin Agreement between the Ottoman Empire and Iran in 1639. The

Qasr-i Chirin Agreement was signed in a period when the concept of nationhood did not exist. The Kurds were simply one among many other ethnic groups divided between larger political entities. The borders, moreover, separated the empires but not the populations. Their symbolic significance was greater than their practical significance, and they lacked any popular or mass ideological value since they reflected dynastic polities and not purportedly popular ones. Not only was the civil population able to continue crossing the borders, but also some Kurdish chieftains or emirs even enjoyed privileged status in both empires. These chieftains could even manage to change their formal allegiance to suit their short-term interests without provoking a strong reaction from either Tehran or Constantinople.

During the second division of Kurdistan in the 1920s, however, the question of borders was directly linked to that of nationhood. The Kurds clearly understood that the new division implied the splitting up of *their* nation and regarded it as a betrayal by the Kemalist state of its early promises to protect the Kurds at any cost. Moreover, the newly established borders were militarized. For the new states, as well as for Iran, the borders not only separated the state entities between them, but also became symbols of their separate national entities and economies. Crossing the borders without authorization henceforth meant betraying a nation-state. For the Kurds, communication among family and tribe members could thus only be maintained by militarily challenging the borders and the national sovereignties that the borders represented.

A second reason for the tension between the Kurds and the nation-states is found in the states' nationalism. In Iran and Iraq, the state-nationalism inadvertently stimulated and strengthened the then rather weak Kurdish nationalism as a response. The situation was more explosive in Turkey, since as early as 1924 the state embraced Turkish nationalism as an official doctrine. As numerous official statements attest, non-Turkish speakers were identified *ipso facto* as potential enemies of the Turkish nation. Language, as the criterion of distinction between majority and minority, between "us" and the "others," replaced the previous religious distinctions. Moreover, Turkish nationalism, as it was officially propagated in the Republic's semi-official organs, switched rapidly from a cultural nationalism towards a social-Darwinist one that explained the relations between Turkishness and Kurdishness as an eternal fight between a positive, progressive, and civilized culture and a negative, reactionary, and barbarian atavism.

Both Kemalist intellectuals and military officers came to regard the Kurds as a feudal ethno-class that had to be assimilated or destroyed for the sake of both state security and social progress.[29] Anatolian history was rapidly Turkicised. The official history denied the existence of other components and banned the assertion of other cultural or ethnic identities.[30] This repression was in complete contradiction to the premises of the War of Independence, which was explicitly conducted in the name of the Kurdish-Turkish fraternity.

The third reason was specific to Turkey, where, following the foundation of the Turkish Republic, the Kemalist government abandoned its promises to protect the Caliphate and preserve Islam as the basis of the new state. The state's official renunciation of Islam caused further deterioration in relations with the Kurds. Moreover, coercive westernization did not lead to the democratization of the country or to political modernity. On the contrary, it strengthened the authoritarian nature of the Kemalist regime. Such reforms as the forcible imposition of western dress, the banning of the religious brotherhoods, and the attempt to replace Islam with a Kemalist civil religion created strong reactions in the Kurdish regions and in many other regions of Turkey. The state responded in turn with greater coercion, and in 1925 with mass executions. Conservative Kurdish circles regarded these measures as an indefensible direct state intervention in the religious and private spheres and as more evidence of the betrayal of the initial Kemalist promises.

These three factors—national feeling, border realignments, and Turkish secularism—provoked strong reactions among the Kurds. From the 1920s to the mid-1940s, a series of revolts took place in Iran, Iraq, and Turkey. These violent contests marked the transition from primitive rebellions to modern forms of violence, such as guerrilla warfare conducted by political-military organizations, aiming at the constitution of a Kurdish nation-state. Although none of the Kurdish revolts succeeded in mobilizing the entire Kurdish population in any single country, almost all of them gave birth to trans-border, region-wide military mobilizations. The trans-border nature of the families, tribes, and religious brotherhoods, which have been divided by the arbitrary nature of borders, facilitated this region-wide mobilization. But the Kurdish nationalist intelligentsia, which had formerly resided mainly in Constantinople and which rejected the artificial inter-state borders, also functioned during these decades as a trans-border locus of resistance.

The rebellions of this period brought together two very different types of Kurdish opposition. The first type was embraced by the nationalist Kurdish intelligentsia who rejected the authority of states not because they were states, but because they were non-Kurdish states. Over two decades, this intelligentsia, inheritor of the Kurdish cultural and, later, political nationalism of the late Ottoman period, succeeded in articulating a nationalist discourse and system of symbols and codified Kurdish nationalism by such means as endowing it with a national song, a national flag, a map of Kurdistan, and a national day. Over subsequent decades, all the Kurdish nationalist organizations adopted these unifying symbols. They gave a meaning and concrete manifestation to the idea of Kurdishness. The nationalist opposition from the 1920s through the 1940s developed and elaborated a case for an independent Kurdish state, or at least for the autonomy of the Kurdish regions in the three countries.

A second branch of opposition was that of the Kurdish chieftains and religious brotherhoods. It did not reject the states because they were Turkish, Syrian, Iraqi, or Iranian states, but simply because they were *states* and, as states, they imposed territorial control, taxation, and military recruitment. The new states, in fact, identified the tribes and brotherhoods as obstacles to the goal of centralized and modernized rule and targeted them as institutions to be transformed or eliminated. The Turkish state and, to a somewhat lesser degree, the Iranian state went so far as to label the tribes and brotherhoods as repressive feudal institutions accountable for the social "backwardness" of the country—and even the whole Muslim world. The tribes and the brotherhoods, accustomed to moving about freely, also contested the new state borders and the militarization of those borders. Simply to maintain the unity of tens of thousands of divided families and of hundreds of tribes now required the ongoing and habitual transgressing of borders and challenging of the state authorities.

These two branches of opposition possessed neither the same social origins nor the same aspirations. But progressively they fused and gave birth to a single opposition. While the nationalist intelligentsia

31

acceded reluctantly to an alliance with these rural forces that it had previously accused of being reactionary, those same forces had begun gradually to embrace nationalism, finding in the nationalist discourse and symbols a political syntax that could legitimize their own struggle. As a result, the rebellions could tap the human resources of both the Kurdish intelligentsia and Kurds with military experience in the national armies to create a capable military-political leadership.

The successful repression of the rebellions required at times regional cooperation between the states of Syria, Iraq, Iran, Turkey, and, at least in the case of the Ararat rebellion in 1930, the Soviet Union. In fact, these states assumed that the Kurdish nationalism was a threat to the regional status quo, and therefore to the security of each one of them. The defeat of the rebellions led to a "period of silence" and profound fatigue among the Kurdish populations. This passivity continued from the end of the autonomous self-proclaimed Mahabad Republic in Iran (1946) to the beginning of the Barzani rebellion in 1961.

The rebellions of the 1920s through the 1940s did, however, did transmit a pattern of uprising to future generations. Armed struggle against the states had become an ingrained part of individual and collective memories, and the very high casualties (especially in Turkey, where tens of thousands of civilians had been killed) linked this memory of rebellion to the duty for revenge. In addition, the period of rebellions was also the period of the codification of the nationalist doctrine and symbols, and future generations, influenced by these symbols, could perceive themselves to be participants in a historically continuous resistance. They could thus project themselves as *the* generation charged with the mission to lead this movement to victory and set an example for coming generations.

The Third Era of the Kurdish Movement:
Towards New Forms of Violence

The period of silence ended with the military coup d'état in Iraq in 1958. In the wake of the political changes, Mullah Mustafa Barzani, a prominent figure in the Kurdish nationalist movement during the 1930s and 1940s, was allowed to return to Iraq. The Kurdistan Democratic Party, of which Barzani was the symbolic leader, decided in 1961 to launch a new rebellion to win autonomy for the Kurdish regions. This uprising continued until its failure in 1975. Just a few months after the end of this rebellion, a second one erupted and lasted until the establishment of a Kurdish "Safe Haven" in northern Iraq in 1991.

To some extent, the 1961 uprising conformed to the traditional pattern of Kurdish uprisings in the first part of the twentieth century and brought together the rural opposition and the educated elite with a modern education. But unlike previous resistance, it brought about two decisive changes in Kurdish politics. The first concerns the place of the urban centers and populations in the armed struggle. During the first half of the twentieth century, the intelligentsia was surprisingly isolated from the urban populations. The Kurdish towns in Turkey, for instance, did not participate in the uprisings, largely because the influential Kurdish urban intelligentsia of that country actually lived in exile in Syria and Lebanon. In Iraq and in Iran, urban populations supported the nationalist ideas, but they did not constitute the main force of the nationalist struggle. During the Barzani uprising, however, not only the intelligentsia, but also many other segments of urban populations, particularly the youth, became radicalized. The mountain-based leadership of the uprising was not cut off from the urban residents.

The second change attributable to the 1961 uprising is the new heterogeneity of the motivations and dreams of those who participated in the rebellion. Although Barzani, and the leadership of the uprising in general, had rather conservative and pro-Western positions, the fighters and militants who participated in the uprising possessed different social origins and worldviews. While Kurdish nationalism provided the fundamental motives for the mobilization of all the fighters, the younger urban militants were also heavily influenced by what we might call revolutionary romanticism. To describe the uprising, they coined the neologism *chorech*, a word that hereafter would mean revolution in the Kurdish language.

Like the concept *chorech*, the figure of the "militant" was also almost totally foreign to the tradition of Kurdish nationalism. Previously, the Westernized Kurdish intelligentsia were known as *effendis* and were counted among the urban dignitaries..[31] The *effendis* originated from the wealthy old urban families that dominated the economic and political life of the cities. Educated in Western schools or in Western manners, they became familiar with nationalist ideas and aimed at the integration of the Kurdish nation as a distinct entity into modern civilization; they acted not as militants of a struggle, but rather as the enlightened strata of the urban milieu.

Few of the militants of the 1960s, on the other hand, came from the old wealthy families. They were often very young, high school or first-year university students. Very few of them were educated in Western countries. They became familiar with nationalist ideas through the Kurdish collective memory and rapidly assimilated the Kurdish nationalist symbolism. The nationalism of these militants embraced, however, more than national emancipation; it went hand in hand with the socialist ideas and visions of society that were part of the hopes and illusions of a rapidly changing Middle East.

One can thus easily understand why the uprising gave birth to a radicalization that was far more left-leaning than what the very conservative Barzani could either tolerate or halt. This radicalization affected even Iraqi Kurdistan, where under the official banner of the Democratic Party of Kurdistan many leftist tendencies coexisted and could only be controlled thanks to Barzani's personal influence (one of those tendencies, however, later metamorphosed into open dissidence). But very soon, Barzani's uprising became the starting point of a Kurdish radicalism that spread to Iran and Turkey. In those two countries, yet another factor facilitated the nationalist radicalization of Kurdish youth: the spread of left-wing ideas among the youth through the underground in Iran and through a more open and democratic environment in Turkey.

At its beginning this radicalization was in no way violent. Although it cultivated a revolutionary romanticism and drew on the popular imagery of the guerrilla warfare waged by the left wing in Latin America and Asia, it aspired almost exclusively to turn the youth themselves into actors and legitimize the minimal claims of Kurdish nationalism. Even by the end of the 1960s, the claims of the Kurdish nationalist intellectuals did not go beyond administrative and/or cultural autonomy for the Kurds in these two countries.

Just over one decade later, however, the transition from a pacific, left-leaning cultural nationalism to an entrenched acceptance of violence appeared inevitable. Many factors contribute to this transformation. First of all, a significant gap remained between the rhetoric of revolutionary romanticism of the Kurdish nationalist circles and the enforced passivity in which the young generations found themselves. By the end of the 1970s, at least some sections of the Iranian and the Turkish left had embraced the strategy of armed struggle, and thereby also radicalized the Kurdish youth, especially in the urban areas. Second, this radicalized youth had arrived at the conclusion that non-violent means of action were ineffective. Indeed, in Iran, the regime of the Shah had only become more repressive, making almost any form of legal opposition impossible. In Turkey, not only were activities on behalf of all Kurdish claims, including those related to the simple recognition of the language, punished with jail time, but also the severe repression following the military coup in 1971 demonstrated the frailty of the democratic framework. Both countries criminalized any claim of ethnic or cultural identity and solidarity. The inability of young Kurds to negotiate their integration without completely re-nouncing their Kurdishness consequently made violence an attractive option. Finally, as a consequence of the Algiers Agreement of 1975 between Iraq and Iran, the Shah's regime withdrew its support from the Barzani uprising, thus leading to the uprising's collapse and to real shock among the Kurds, including those of Iran and Turkey. The end of this uprising, which had become the central reference point for nationalist Kurdish aspirations, created both a deep frustration and a vacuum. Both in Iran and in Turkey, Kurdish militants were eager to start a new movement that could fill this vacuum and, with a new mobilization, give meaning to the whole of Kurdish history in the twentieth century.

It was under these circumstances that, in 1977–78, two new Kurd-ish organizations were founded in Turkey: the PKK and the KUK (National Liberators of Kurdistan). They both saw themselves as the new standard bearers of the Kurdish cause throughout the Middle

East, and both decided to start armed struggles immediately with the construction of a unified and socialist Kurdistan as their ultimate goal. A comprehensive history of these two movements has yet to be written. But a quick overview shows that they recruited mainly from among the rural youth that had been radicalized during the 1970s and from among those whose parents had recently immigrated to the towns. Their social base was very different from that of the westernized nationalist intelligentsia of 1920s and from that of the early left-leaning intelligentsia of the 1960s. They were poorly educated, and though boys formed the great majority, many girls also participated. They possessed poor prospects for economic and political integration. Militancy and the Kurdish movement offered to many of them an alternative to unemployment or, for the girls, a way to achieve a degree of dignity and emancipation. The romanticism of armed struggle, with which they had been familiar almost from birth, constituted the only intellectual framework they had. In the conditions of the generalized violence of Turkey in the 1970s they embraced violence swiftly. But during the initial years of their activity, the violence they directed against the state remained marginal. Aiming at the monopolization of the Kurdish political sphere, and depending mainly on the same social basis (first-generation urban youth as well as rural youth), their violence acquired a fratricidal aspect, pitting young Kurdish nationalists who shared the same aspirations against each other. The organizations committed, according to some estimates, more than 400 killings of Kurds. Only the PKK managed to survive the period of military rule and mount a guerrilla war against the Turkish state.

Although the same romantic visions of armed struggle were popular among the Kurdish youth in Iran, the situation evolved very differently there. The popular revolution of 1979 mobilized the Kurdish as well as Iranian urban populations. By February 1979, the Kurdish movements, both the PDK-I (Democratic Party of Kurdistan-Iran) and the *Komeleh*, were in command of the major Kurdish cities, including Mahabad and Urmiyeh. The Kurdish movement, however, faced a rapidly changing revolution. With the victory of the Islamists over the radical left organizations, the revolution took a more and more stridently monolithic and authoritarian form, rejecting, like the *ancien régime*, the very idea of administrative and cultural autonomy of the minorities. Combat in the cities with government forces led to high losses among the Kurdish movements and compelled them to leave the urban zones and to start a guerrilla war. This war generated internal conflicts, both among the Iranian Kurds themselves and also between them and the Iraqi Kurds.

Finally, in 1975 the sympathizers of Barzani and his opponents in the PUK (Patriotic Union of Kurdistan), a leftist coalition led by Jalal Talabani, began waging a new armed struggle in Iraqi Kurdistan. The withdrawal of American and Iranian support from the Barzani uprising sowed deep mistrust towards the West among the Iraqi Kurds. At the same time, the political and military rapprochement between Baghdad and Moscow made the Kurds much more skeptical of and even hostile toward the Soviet Union. The result for some was a rejection both of communism and of Western democracy that manifested in an increasingly discursive radicalization, with some Iraqi Kurdish groups adopting Maoism as a new universal ideology.

In short, by the end of the 1970s, the Kurdish populations in Iraq, Iran, and Turkey were experiencing either political urban violence or outright guerrilla warfare. The intensity of the violence would only increase over the next two decades.

38

Regional Instability and Domestic Political Arenas
as Sources of Violence

How can we explain this longevity of the Kurdish nationalist organizations, and the forms of violence they used over more than two decades in Turkey, Iran, and Iraq? In fact, several combined factors account for the ability of Kurdish guerrilla organizations in Iraq, Iran, and Turkey to persist and even become primary actors despite losses of tens of thousands of members. Among these factors one should certainly mention the region's general instability. In fact, throughout the 1980s and 1990s, the Middle East has been a battlefield of multiple active or latent inter-state conflicts. The Iran-Iraq War, the tensions between Syria and Iraq and Syria and Turkey, and later the second Gulf War have all created instability throughout the region. The states were thus interested in having allies, including Kurdish ones, in order to exert pressure against their adversaries. While repressing its own Kurds, the Iraqi regime supported the Iranian Kurds. Iran gave similar support to the Iraqi Kurds. Later on, from 1991 to almost the end of the 1990s, Turkey also supported the Iraqi Kurds. Syria gave shelter to the militants of the PKK and allowed the Iraqi Kurds to establish offices in Damascus. Following the military coup in Turkey in 1980, the PKK withdrew its surviving militants from Turkey to Lebanon, where they participated in their first real war: the Israeli-Lebanese war of 1982. These inter-state conflicts marked the end of the individual states' monopoly over the instruments of violence. The Kurdish organizations were only a few of the non-state actors that profited from this evolution.

My impression, however, is that although regional conditions allowed the Kurdish guerrilla organizations to wage armed struggles for a such long period and to find shelter for their decision-making organs, the main reasons for the persistence of violence must ultimately be sought elsewhere, namely in the domestic politics of Iraq, Iran and Turkey. Throughout the 1980s and 1990s, the Iraqi, Iranian, and Turkish regimes remained authoritarian power structures. None of these states, governed or ultimately controlled by non-elected institutions (the Ba'ath Party and increasingly Saddam Hussein himself, the clergy, and the military respectively), created space for the articulation of ethnic identities in politics. They continued to suppress conflicts through the use of coercion and resource allocation rather than resolve them by integrating the combatants into the political process.

A second factor behind the armed struggle of the 1980s and 1990s lies in the Kurdish actors' own perception of their mission. As I stressed earlier, the Kurdish struggle in the late 1970s emerged in large part as a result of a referential vacuum. With the end of the Barzani uprising in 1975, the dominant landmark of the Kurdish political arena disappeared without having been replaced by any prospects for the integration of the Kurds, *qua* Kurds, into the political systems of their respective states. Armed struggle was a means of reinventing a meaning and thereby overcoming this vacuum created by the end of the Barzani rebellion in Iraq.

Moreover, the radicalized Kurdish youth of the late 1970s adopted this task of reinstating a political vision amidst a rapid procession of political events and developments that directly impacted the Kurdish regions in the Middle East. The end of the Barzani uprising, the Iranian revolution and the subsequent repression of the Kurdish movement, the Iran-Iraq war, the use of chemical weapons in Halabdja, the

40

Anfal operations which claimed more than 180,000 Kurdish civilian victims in Iraq, the 1980 military coup d'état in Turkey, the PKK's guerrilla campaign and the state counter-guerrilla campaigns that involved the destruction of thousands of villages and a dozen towns, as well as the assassination of at least two thousand Kurdish intellectuals by "unknown killers"—all these events took place within a time frame of fifteen years. The constantly changing political configurations provided no opportunities for the Kurdish actors to develop alternative strategies to violence, or even to give new directions or dimensions to the policy of violent struggle they were conducting. They acted as dependent components in a region-wide system of violence and were not able to master their own violence, let alone that of the states.

This rapid process of events not only explains the failure of the Kurdish movements to mature and make the switch from violence to peaceful forms of resistance. It also elucidates why throughout the 1980s and 1990s they found it so difficult to give a sense to their own past and their future, and as a consequence, why they are virtually forced to conduct their policies day-to-day without any mid- or long-term strategic perspective.

There is, in fact, a close relation between the meaning that individuals and communities are able to give to their past and their capacity to perceive the present and the future as meaningful time-scales. An extremely violent past filled with consequential developments and events precludes individuals and collectivities (families, circles of friends, villages, urban populations, etc.) from mentally organizing their immediate history into comprehensible and meaningful experiences separated by clear-cut temporal landmarks. Amidst a dizzyingly rapid procession of incidents such as occurred in the 1980s and the 1990s, the past becomes a confused ensemble of tragic events that follow one after the other and resist mental classification. These events were obviously in themselves very important and possessed a meaning within their contemporary horizons when they occurred, not least because each of them provoked hundreds, if not thousands, of deaths. But almost none of them constituted an *episode*—a time-period whose beginning and end are marked by significant events, allowing subjects to put their own past into a positive framework, or at least, convincing themselves that a dramatic past is over with. The large number of events and their very violent nature prevented Kurdish society, movements and militants—as well as Turkish, Iraqi and Iranian societies—from assigning constructive meanings to the events and then arranging them into a hierarchy of meaning.

This inability to fix past-oriented landmarks also impedes the imagining of a constructive future, i.e. a future as a time-scale in which projects can be conceived and realized and programs proposed and fulfilled. Instead, the immediate future is perceived as merely another period during which multiple tragic events will certainly occur, and, as in the past, individuals and collectivities will not be able to provide a constructive meaning to them. This impossibility of giving coherence to the past and of projecting the future in a constructive imagination also diminishes the coherence of the present. The present is not conceived of as a link between an understood past and a foreseeable immediate or mid-term future, but simply as the moment in which one lives, acts, and tries to survive. The repeated acts of mass violence and war should be seen as cause and effect of a profound readjustment of the individuals' and collectivities' very conception of time.

So although the Kurdish movements managed to persist through the 1980s and 1990s, the price for this survival was a strong disruption in the very perception of time. The Kurdish movements, as well as many Kurds as individuals or members of a given social group, have suffered from this dissasociation between the past, the future and, therefore, the present. In many cases, it has led to fatalism and autism, or to the simple overriding goal of survival in the present.[32] But among the Kurds of Turkey, it also led to new forms of violence, namely self-sacrificial ones.

The Turkish Exception

Why did sacrificial forms of violence emerge among the Kurds in Turkey and not among those of the other countries? Answering this question requires that one analyze the peculiar case of Turkey and the evolution of the Kurdish movement in this country.

Turkey in the 1980s and the 1990s presented a paradoxical situation (which continues at the beginning of the third millennium). On one hand, Turkey had, to some extent at least, an institutional democratic framework and was obviously more open to the outside world than Iran, Syria, or Iraq. On the other hand, Turkey is the only multi-party country in the world to have an official state-cult—Kemalism—with its temple *Anıtkabir*, the tomb where Mustafa Kemal's mortal remains rest, and its "Temple-Keepers," the military and civil bureaucracy. Although Kemalism as a system or blueprint of social and political organization became an anachronism decades ago, it remains the constitutionally obligatory world vision for Turkey's citizens. The Temple-Keepers are still charged with deciding if a political position is acceptable, or if it constitutes "deviance," or even "perversity."[33] Moreover, as Şerif Mardin has suggested, "'the hidden hand' or 'conspiracy' theory often passes for a philosophy of history in contemporary Turkey."[34] This political culture and its historical, cultural, and psychological dimensions have yet to be fully analyzed. But the quest for unanimism, the basic foundation of the Kemalist cult, led to the criminalization of any kind of division and to the designation of any defender of an alternative meaning and policy (communists, Kurdish nationalists, Islamists, and, in some periods, liberal intellectuals, etc.) as internal enemies. Paradoxically enough, the more the country became integrated into the world economy and European political structures, the more the political culture adopted an autarkic character.

These conditions also determined the evolution of the Kurdish issue in Turkey, not only in the first decades of the Republic, but also during the last two decades. The state deliberately wielded massive coercion against any kind of Kurdish legal political representation and consequently stifled any prospects for a political solution to this question, whose very existence is still denied. Ever since the foundation of the Republic, and particularly since the beginning of the PKK's guerrilla warfare, in fact, the official Turkish policy has always denied the very existence of the Kurds as a distinct group and qualified the Kurdish claims and struggles either as separatist or as terrorist. Thus, it is no wonder that the Kurdish spokespersons for a non-violent, political solution have been banned as "internal enemies."[35] In spite of the emphatic insistence of the reformist Turgut Özal that his program could stop the war and allow the integration of Kurdish political actors, the official state policy never changed.

Space does not permit me to describe this policy in detail.[36] It is however important to stress that throughout the last two decades the Kurdish issue has been at the heart of both state coercion and power relations in Turkey. The state's strategy of social engineering through successive crises and its requirement of absolute loyalty against "separatism" and "terrorism" created the conditions for a permanent mobilization of Turkish nationalists. It also allowed the rehabilitation of the Kemalist hegemonic discourse, which had become widely contested at the end of the 1980s. The military, but also many left- and right-wing politicians and intellectuals who had previously criticized the existence of any "official ideology," including Kemalism, believed that the Turkish nation needed a strong shield, allowing a constant mobilization against "terrorist separatism" (and "reactionary Islamism"). Kemalism was precisely that armor. But as I will explain in the second chapter, as a justification of conflict, the Kurdish question was also a cost-effective pawn, not least because it allowed different bureaucratic constituencies within the state to negotiate their part in the processes of resource allocation and legitimization. Thanks to its position in fighting the PKK's guerrillas, the army, although divided, remained the most important power structure of the country. As in many other cases in the world, the situation in Turkey during the 1980s and 1990s constituted a remarkable confirmation of Tilly's model of war as an instrument of state building[37] or of intra-state power-building.

I should also add that, alongside massive coercion, the Turkish state employed symbolic violence on a broad scale throughout the 1980s and 1990s. This violence was very different from what Pierre Bourdieu understood by "symbolic violence": the internalization of the mechanisms of domination and submission.[38] In Turkey, as in many other places, the symbolic violence prepared, legitimized, and allowed the continuation of the physical violence. It led to the dehumanization of the Kurds, "neutralizing" the crimes committed against them and their identity.

Taken together, these elements shed much light on the reasons why the state's coercion was so massive in the Kurdish regions. They account for more than 30,000 of the almost 40,000 deaths that the war caused. They explain also why many Kurdish young people no longer feared death, which had become de facto and omnipresent, and why violence could remain so attractive to them throughout almost two decades.

The PKK: From National Liberation to the Invention of the "New Kurd"

But it is also important to take into account the PKK's symbolic universe, its internal structures, and its evolution. These elements also account for the continuation of violence. They explain why some PKK members and sympathizers whom the party could not control switched from a rational/instrumental form of violence to nihilistic and sacrificial kinds of violence and challenged the party's own decisions by organizing suicide-attacks or immolating themselves.

First of all, one should remember that ever since its foundation in 1978, i.e., long before it became a structured guerrilla movement, the PKK has offered a field of socialization to Kurdish youth of very modest origins. To be sure, by the end of the 1970s, much of the Kurdish population no longer welcomed this socialization. Kurdish parents—much like the parents of the Turkish militants involved in violence—certainly accepted a kind of "socio-psychological" moratorium with their rebel children[39]: i.e., they accepted that for a while, the youth had the right to use violence as a form of expression, socialization, and maturation. But they did it in anger, not least because the PKK's praxis had thrown the formerly peaceful Kurdish regions into violence. Like the majority of Turks, many Kurds had also welcomed the 1980 military coup d'état that put an end to the violence. Some families even denounced their own children to the state authorities in the hope that in prison, at least, their children would be safer and would be released within a couple of years.

But the military regime committed a grave mistake: while stopping the violence, it also destroyed a field of socialization and did not replace it with a new, pacified one that could include symbolic resources of Kurdishness. To the contrary, it saw all manifestations of Kurdishness, including the language, as social illnesses to be cured with an overdose of Kemalism. To a society that was less and less ready to accept the rhetorical notion of the "happiness of being Turks,"[40] the military regime offered more and more Turkishness as the condition of its survival. The result was that a much more radicalized socialization process started, but this process took place underground, mostly among boys aged 10 to 15. When the PKK decided to start its guerrilla campaign in 1984, many of these young boys (and some girls) welcomed this new phase of violence as a means of the re-conquest of their symbolic resources and their Kurdish identity and as the starting point of a new and violent, but nevertheless open, process of socialization. The new situation was in fact a paradoxical one. On the one hand, the PKK was a clandestine organization, its members being massively arrested or killed by the security forces; on the other hand, these militants acted quite openly within the Kurdish society, using at once the sympathy that the Kurdish population had for them, and violence to obtain the neutrality and silence of their opponents. Thus, in many villages and towns, they could replace the state-appointed judges, teachers and fiscal services.

The PKK was initially a product of the widespread violence of Turkey in the 1970s.[41] As a leftist organization, it had been influenced by the contemporary Marxist vulgate and the success of the guerrilla movements in Africa and Asia during that decade. "Marxism," as broadly defined, provided the PKK with a universal syntax of legitimization. Like some other minority groups' (e.g. the Basques') nationalisms, Kurdish nationalism found in Marxism a pre-packaged ideology that allowed it to legitimize the "particular" in terms of the "universal," the national with the international. Under the peculiar conditions of 1970–1980s Turkey, this Marxism, however, possessed a Fanonian dimension. Insofar as violence was conceived as the very condition of the emergence of a new man, *homo kurdicus*, that violence could not be limited to a tangible goal. Rather, Öcalan himself explained on many occasions that the principal goal of the violence was not national liberation or even the simple construction of a socialist entity (a Kurdish state or a federation of socialist republics of the Middle East), but rather the destruction of the "enslaved," and therefore hateful, Kurdish personality.[42] The Party, in fact, did not fix a goal either for its members or for the Kurds broadly speaking (on the contrary, as in the case of Franz Fanon, victory itself seemed a frightening prospect[43]). Rather, it emphasized the fact that true liberation would come from an inward purification and an absolute fidelity to the martyrs and to the "Serok" (leader). Violence was not simply a means allowing the liberation of Kurdistan; it was a guiding principle of emancipating the Kurdish individuality. Therefore, it had to produce more inward effects than the outward ones.

If the PKK was influenced by Marxism, it was also, paradoxically, profoundly influenced by the Turkish state cult of Kemalism. In fact, the success of the PKK was largely due to its capacity to learn from the State and appropriate its systematic symbolism to Kurdish ends. It was able to replace the "Eternal Leader," as Mustafa Kemal is known in Turkey, with a Kurdish "Leader" (later abstracted to "Leadership," and then, finally, the "Sun of the Kurds"). The Kurdish "people-trans-formed-into-an-army" replaced the nation-army praised by Turkish textbooks. The party's flag replaced the Turkish star and crescent. The party's "tribunals," "tax-rollers," and military recruiters were accepted as manifestations of a would-be Kurdish state. Like the Kemalist ideo-logues, the PKK also rejected the known past and proposed a return to an imagined "Golden Age." Only this uncorrupted Golden Age could give birth to the future, and therefore allow the renewal of a history that had been interrupted by the corruption of the past. For the Kemal-ists, Ergenekon, the mythic land of the Turks, was the place where this Golden Age had taken place. In response, Mesopotamia became the imagined land of the Kurds, the place of the Kurdish Golden Age and of Kawa the Blacksmith, the mythic Kurdish hero. At last, young Kurds had a code and system of symbols equivalent to those of the Turks and with that, a degree of spiritual and social equality. At its best, even if its rhetoric strikes Western ears as bombastic and propa-gandistic, the PKK genuinely sought to restore dignity to a generation of impressionable youth.

Nationalist Mysticism, Bureaucracy, and Martyrdom

This symbolic universe in which the PKK members and sympa-thizers evolved explains why, for almost 20 years, and in spite of very heavy causalities—at least 30,000 fighters died in combat—the PKK never failed to find candidates to train as new guerrillas. The PKK, whose very first years were marked by violence and internal coercion, was structured around Abdullah Öcalan's charismatic personality.[44]

During the initial years of guerrilla warfare, Öcalan lived not in Turkey but either in his flat in Damascus or in the party's training camps in Lebanon's Bekaa Valley, and this geographic and symbolic inaccessibility was key to his mystique. For the increasing numbers of his sympathizers, and particularly the young boys and girls in Turkey, he was the distant demiurge about whom anything could be imagined; the one who, one day, would come back as the victorious messiah. Until that day, however, he would exist as an almost non-material incarnation of Kurdishness. For the growing ranks of trainee fighters in the Bekaa Valley, however, he was at once material and physically close. Obviously, he was the *Serok*, or "Leader." But he used to have a picture taken with every new fighter, and lectured in person often. It was thus possible for Kurds to overcome the distance and time that separated them from their Leader—but only on condition of becoming guerrilla fighters. Achieving proximity to the "Leader," even on these terms, became the dream of thousands of young Kurds.

Öcalan's charisma developed and was institutionalized throughout the 1980s. After almost one decade of institutionalization, however, the party inevitably lost its original character of a big, unified family. It had grown into a much more complex organization, one that resembled a three-level pyramid. Öcalan constituted the top level of the pyramid. He was a part-mystic, part-rational, part-material, part-ideal figure and could constantly slide from a kind of religious and romantic discourse to a very rational one. His multi-volume *Analysis* (*Cözümlemeler*) proposed no tactical or strategic direction to the militants but rather related his life story and his perception of the world. Significantly, this inward-looking work encouraged his sympathizers to focus not on state-building but on a kind of species-building of a new enlightened *homo Kurdicus*. This new species, the vehicle of the new "Kurdish humanism" of the coming Golden Age, would derive its meaning primarily through Öcalan himself, the ultimate source of wisdom and love, and secondarily through the class of martyrs, the premiere exemplars of the new race.

The martyrs were a part of the "Leadership," in other words, of the mystical body of Öcalan himself. As I noted above, during the first decade of fighting, each guerrilla-trainee had a photo taken with the "Leader"; this photograph, demonstrating the fighter's proximity to the heart of the movement, was published only after the fighter's death. Accordingly, the fighters, now martyrs, were buried not with sorrow and tears, but with joy. But over the years, the number of the trainees increased considerably and it became logistically impossible for each one to get a picture taken with a more and more itinerant Öcalan, who shuttled often between Damascus and the Bekaa Valley. The later martyrs thus ceased to enjoy the same status as the earlier ones. The most esteemed circle was composed of the martyrs of the first years, those who had taken part in the saga from its very beginning and thus shared in Öcalan's charisma. The second circle was composed of young boys and girls who joined the movement at the turn of the 1990s, but who were still close enough to Öcalan, then still accessible to his militants.

Öcalan, "who fought for the honor of the martyrs and for the future," did not consider himself accountable to his time, nor to the existing Kurds, but only to history, i.e. to the coming Kurdishness of the future, the goal for which the martyrs fall. In fact, after being the "Leader" for a couple of years, he changed his status and became the "Leadership." As the "Leadership," incarnating the "martyrs," the Kurdish national cause, and the future, Öcalan could promote some military commands, dismiss others, first approve and thereafter sanction by death some of their acts, accuse his militants of cowardice and villainy, and use very derogatory words to describe the Kurdish people. Yet by 1993, he seemed to grasp the failure of his leadership and the necessity to adopt more pragmatic programs that would improve his image in both Turkey and in Europe (many European countries, among them Germany and France, considered the PKK a terrorist organization and outlawed its activities), and also among the Iraqi and Iranian Kurds. By adopting a new flexible line, the PKK sought to be accepted as a rational, i.e., credible, organization, fighting only in order to improve the fate of the Kurds in Turkey. Pragmatism meant that Öcalan would stop fighting with the Iraqi Kurds who were trying to establish their own autonomous region in Iraq after the Gulf War, and would begin negotiating with the Turkish state. This last objective appeared attainable since Turgut Özal, the Turkish president, had asked him through the mediation of some Kurdish figures such as Talabani to declare a cease-fire.[45]

But this move toward pragmatic policies was also related to the internal transformations of the PKK. During the 1980s and 1990s, the multiplication of its activities required the PKK to establish a bureaucratic apparatus within the party itself, in Kurdistan, and in Europe among the diaspora. This apparatus, which constituted the second level of the party's power structures, was a rational, enterprise-minded one. It was made up of the military "commanders" who employed severe internal coercion on Öcalan's behalf,[46] and of the elder respected Kurdish nationalists[47] who had joined the PKK at the end of the 1980s. During the 1980s, in fact, the PKK was perceived by many former Kurdish nationalists who have been militating during the 1960s and 1970s, and by many Kurdish intellectuals, as an adventurer or even as a dangerous organization. By the end of this decade, however, some

52

of them decided to join the "national struggle" conducted by it. This reinforcement allowed the PKK to improve its image and to present itself as the perpetrator of a century-long Kurdish struggle. Moreover, the newcomers were able to elaborate a moderate, dialogue-seeking discourse and program, which was more readily heard both in Turkey and in Europe.[48] The relations between these civil bureaucrats, who were active mainly in the diplomatic field in Europe and in the legal-civil organizations in Turkey, on one hand, and party's military commanders, on the other, were marked by conflict. Many aging commanders, who had been fighting as guerrillas since 1984, adopted the strategy of continuing the war at any cost. Some of them considered the war both as a national duty and as a means of establishing their own territorial "zones," where they had an absolute autonomy. At least some of the commanders conducted policies of "privatized violence" quite independent of Öcalan's direction. Öcalan had no way to control the activities of these autonomous "lordships" constructed within his own party. However, other bureaucrats, chiefly the civilian ones, were eager to end the violence. Their age, their status, and their long experience as militants, bureaucrats, or "diplomats" in Europe pushed them to evolve from revolutionary romanticism and the party's official dogma towards more pragmatic strategies that could offer them a political career inside Turkey. A peace that could insure the recognition of the "hard core" symbols of Kurdishness, namely recognition of the Kurdish language and culture, was, and still remains, the main goal of this category of Kurdish activist.

The lowest level of the pyramid was continuously rejuvenated by the disciples of the "Messiah." These young, ardent, ill-educated followers, many born after the party's founding in 1978, typically joined the movement of their own volition and saw themselves as Öcalan's personal defenders. They had only a mythologized vision of the Party's first two decades of struggles. Long accustomed to the burials of the martyrs, which had been transformed into national festivities, the newcomers had no fear of dying. The party's mystic discourse and symbols galvanized them but left them ignorant of the party's internal power relations and structures. Apart from songs and images on videocassettes, the party's press organs were the only cultural resource made available to them. This cultural resource was a sectarian one. It included extremely long and confused articles written without theses, but repeating a codified and very limited stock of words. Already even today, just a couple years after the end of the war, understanding these writings requires a specific hermeneutic; their very semantic construction held a meaning only then and only for the believers. Like most cult literature, the texts alternate between promises and threats, filling their readers at once with darkness and hope.

These cultural resources performed a simultaneously frightening and a hope-restoring function. They put an emphasis on personal responsibility and perfection, obtainable exclusively through deeper initiation in texts such as Öcalan's *Analysis* and through the development of the spirit of self-sacrifice. Personal responsibility itself was not understood in a positive, self-improving manner but required that one accept the complete destruction of his or her personality in order to fuse with the abstract collective personality of the PKK—a process chillingly known as "being PKK'cised" (*PKK'leşme*). It involved responsibility, but this responsibility meant that one was constantly perched on an edge, always in imminent danger of falling. Nobody knew exactly what the criteria were for "failing" or for not attaining the assigned objective. Öcalan alone, and with an infallible precision, knew who had "fallen down." But for the rank-and-file militants, falling down was something at once frightening and enigmatic. One could have fallen down without even being aware of it. There were no landmarks, signposts, or barriers that could signal that one remained safely on the edge or had already fallen down. Fidelity to Öcalan and an exclusive love for him was obviously a criterion, but at the same time there could be no guarantee that one's "real" intentions were good.

The party's press and Öcalan's *Analysis* were in fact posing more questions to the militants (and sympathizers) than providing answers. The questions themselves were expressed in religious terminology: How could one be certain that one's love for Öcalan would be accepted as a pure one and not as an act of hypocrisy (*münafiklik*)? And how could one be sure in one's heart that one's love *truly* was pure and not an illusion? How could one be certain that, tomorrow, this true and pure love would not be followed by a betrayal? Did not Öcalan himself repeat that many people thought that they truly loved him, but they were deceiving him, or they did not love him in the real manner, or that, in spite of this love, they were ready to betray him at any moment? Did he not give many concrete examples of such betrayals? Being willing to die for the party and for Öcalan was obviously was one of the conditions of pure love, but Öcalan himself repeated that death was not enough, because it could constitute a kind of evasion.

By the 1990s, while the PKK bureaucracy was developing steadily more rational and pragmatic policies, the party itself was coming to resemble a purely religious sect, asking for faith rather than for conviction, inviting one to embrace the true faith rather than to fight for a national goal. It kept its "believers" constantly aware that they could topple over the precipice into betrayal. In the tragic situation of the 1990s, when thousands of fighters were dying each year and the

Turkish army was destroying thousands of villages, the PKK's fighters found themselves without any positive landmark that could give a meaning to their fight and allow them to envisage a future. The party's charisma-based cognitive and symbolic universe could not lead to the construction of a "positive subject." In a devastated material and symbolic framework, Öcalan remained as the only landmark and the only path to follow. He was the only positive element in an otherwise completely dark and corrupted picture. The sacralization of Öcalan's person was the condition of the growth and efficiency of the party.

Not only was this sole warrant of non-negotiable purity and non-compromising integrity increasingly in physical danger from the Turkish authorities, but during the 1990s the PKK itself was changing direction. The party's bureaucracy—and Öcalan himself—understood clearly that either the guerrilla war should be stopped in order to make room for other modes of action, or the scope and scale of violence should be stepped up. Although they probably possessed the material and human resources to widen the violence, they feared its unpredictable consequences. Abandoning the armed struggle and switching to political resistance was the only alternative remaining. The PKK's leadership circles were already debating this alternative before the capture of Öcalan. But for the militants and their sympathizers such an option required compromises, and compromises would deprive the party of its mysticism. There was an unavoidable tension between pragmatism and the mindset in which the PKK's fighters and sympathizers were trained. Under these circumstances, the hunt for Öcalan and his eventual arrest meant that the fighters and sympathizers lost the last remaining landmark they had had.

This tension was unbearable. In a shortened time-horizon where the past had no meaning other than corruption, where the Turkish state accepted no prospect of a peaceful solution that would allow the militants to project themselves into a meaningful future, the present became devoid of sense. But the worst had yet to come: Öcalan's arrest, and his first statements in captivity, statements that resembled a form of repentance, created a vacuum of meaning for the party's emotionally distressed militants and sympathizers. The threats against Öcalan's life and the PKK's moves toward pragmatism destroyed the remaining landmarks. For many, self-suppression became the only option. Without Öcalan life had no meaning, and it also could not have any meaning with a capitulating or compromising PKK.

Some party members and many of its sympathizers therefore chose death. Insistent pressure from the party's leadership on the sympathizers finally put an end to the suicidal attacks and the acts of self-immolation. The militants and sympathizers were, most probably, given assurances that Öcalan had not betrayed them and that he would survive. But the evolution of this movement—from violence as means of construction of a field of socialization, to a rational violence as a means of power-building, and finally to the nihilist self-sacrificial forms of violence—offers an instructive example for understanding the evolution of violence in other parts of the Middle East and the world.

CHAPTER TWO

From Political Struggle to Self-Sacrifice

Violence in Turkey

On September 10, 2001, a left-wing militant detonated a bomb he was bearing on his body. When he blew himself up he killed two police officers and injured several other policemen. This attack was only the latest in a long series of sacrificial acts. As I mentioned in the first chapter, by the end of the 1990s at least thirteen PKK members had blown themselves up and dozens upon dozens of others had immolated themselves. But this latest attack also showed that violence, although weakening, still remains one of the major issues plaguing Turkey. A short chronological overview will suffice to give a sense of the place of violence in recent Turkish history.

Radical left-wing movements arose in Turkey in the wake of the European student movements of 1968, and soon after there were serious clashes between left-wing militants and the security forces. The groups that initiated the armed struggle were formed clandestinely in 1970–71. The military intervention of March 12, 1971 put a temporary end to the violence, but at the cost of massive human rights violations. Then less then one year after the end of military rule in 1973, the fighting between radical left and right militants started again, leading to the deaths of nearly six thousand people between 1974 and 1980. The military intervention of September 12, 1980, which involved an unprecedented level of state coercion, stopped this round of violence for two years. But in the period since the end of that round of military rule, the collective effects of the fighting between different leftist organizations and the security forces, in conjunction with pogroms, death-fasts, and political "assassinations committed by unknown killers" (as the state's authorities officially labeled them) or by the radical Islamist Hizbullah organization, have produced thousands of victims.

Neither culture nor religion nor historical legacy can account for the central place of this violence in Turkish society. Historically speaking, Turkish society has inevitably known some degree of violence. But with the exception of the Kurdish regions, violence occupied only a marginal place in Turkish society in the years between 1923, the date of the founding of the Kemalist Republic, and 1968, the beginning of the student movements. The level of state coercion was also in fact quite low. Although rural and provincial Anatolia in the Kemalist era was an arena of many secret and underground movements,[49] only one of them, that of Menemen in December 1930, gave rise to a violent movement. The state used massive coercion during the so-called "head-dress reform" of 1925, against the unionist and liberal oppositions in 1926, and in the aftermath of the messianic "incident" of Menemen. But except for these periods, the supposed revolutionary violence of the Kemalist State remained limited to the level of rhetoric. Indeed, in 1950, the Republican People's Party (RPP), the former monopoly party, surrendered power peacefully. And the 1960 military coup that led to the execution of the former Prime Minister Adnan Menderes and two of his ministers did not use massive coercion.

Culture also did not play an important role in the emergence and growth of violence. It is true that Turkish popular culture, like many others, cultivates some admiration for certain violent figures who challenge the state (in this case, bandits). A "secret culture" of praise for rebellion against the state has always existed among the Alevi community of Anatolia, and it can also be found among the very diverse population on the Aegean coast. But at the same time, one can also find many elements in the popular culture that extol the values of peaceableness, obedience to authority, and fatalism.

Likewise, religion cannot explain the phenomenon of violence in the country, not least because the majority of left-wing militants in the 1960s and 1970s were openly atheistic and many of the militants of the radical right espoused a pan-Turanist shamanism rather than Islam. Moreover, the official *madhab*, or school of Islamic jurisprudence, of Turkey is the Hanafi *madhab*, the *madhab* known as the most deferential to authority of the four *madhab*s of Sunni Islam. Since the time of Ottoman rule, there has been a close interdependence between religion and the state, wherein the former constantly legitimizes the latter. Finally, even in the 1980s and 1990s only a handful of Turkish Islamist groups resorted to violence, most unlike the case in many Middle Eastern countries. At crucial moments, Islamists in Turkey have almost always opted for submission to the state over violent resistance to it.

Radicalism and Violence: The 1960s and 1970s

Other reasons that have yet to be studied in depth might help to explain the emergence of violence as a massive and chronic phenomenon in Turkey's contemporary political arena. Among them one should mention the population growth that went hand in hand with the constant economic crises and the massive rural exodus that took place from the 1960s until the end of the 1990s. The physical and social shape of the cities changed fundamentally during these decades. The pressures generated by the new arrivals largely marginalized the notable families who used to control the political space in the urban centers.

This rapid urban growth gave birth to a radical youth movement, in the country's main cities (Istanbul, Ankara, and Izmir), but also in many provincial towns. Already by the beginning of the 1960s, the youth movement appeared to be one of the most dynamic forces challenging the established political parties and provincial dynasties. The Kemalist heritage, which charged the youth with the mission of protecting national independence and the goals of the Republican revolution, along with the revolutionary romanticism of the 1960s, played important roles in that generation's perception of itself as a group responsible for the country's future. The mobilization of the youth, which led to an extremely rapid politicization, was a paradoxical one. In the beginning at least, the young students defended the Kemalist principles of "national independence" against "imperialism." According to them, corrupted politicians "in the pay of imperialism" had betrayed the Kemalist revolution. Kemalism, as a doctrine and as a set of discourses and motto, endowed the youth with an almost unquestionable legitimacy. But these young militants faced a state that used other discourses and slogans of the same Kemalist rhetoric to accuse them of being "in the pay of outside enemies and communism."

The state's answer conformed to the premises of the "counterinsurgency" doctrine that was popular in many Asian and Latin American countries during the 1960s and 1970s. The main documents of this doctrine, which were prepared by American counterinsurgency experts, were translated into Turkish and widely taught at the military and police academies. They openly advocated the violation of human rights, including "plundering, massacres and rape," as legitimate means of "psychological warfare."[50] Already by the second half of the 1960s the army formed a special organization called the *Özel Harp Dairesi* (the Bureau of Special Warfare), more commonly known as *Kontrgerilla*. The domino theory of the export and expansion of communism to Third World countries was a central tenet of this doctrine.

The adoption of such a doctrine inevitably led to the brutal repression of the youth movements. The repressive measures directed at the students intensified during the last two years of the 1960s and were honed to efficiency after the military coup d'état of 1971. The military regime officially proclaimed the radical left organizations to be internal enemies. Three leaders of the revolutionary organizations were formally executed, and tens of others were killed.

The application of the counter-insurgency doctrine, however, only radicalized the left-wing opposition of the youth. It left no room for the student movements to mature and integrate into the political system. After the end of the military regime in 1973, the memory of the slain "martyrs" was sanctified. Many young militants, the "apostles" as one left-wing militant of these years dubs them in his memoirs,[51] swore to avenge the "martyrs" and to follow their path until the victory. The proclamation in 1974 of a general amnesty favoring left-wing militants was not enough to decrease the tension.

The radicalization of the radical right-wing movement led by Colonel Türkeş created a second source of sanctified political violence during the 1960s and 1970s. Although co-opted as an auxiliary force by the state, the radical right movement was also a product of the general politicization of youth. It offered a political syntax to the Turkish-Sunni youth, especially those in central Anatolia, which, like the rest of provincial Turkey, had been marginalized during the Republican decades. The radical right was able to oppose an alternative romanticism of Turkish nationalism, one rooted in Central Asian mythology, to the revolutionary romanticism of the left. Against the project of a socialist Turkey, which the left viewed as the second stage in the natural evolution of the Kemalist revolution, the radical right propounded the ideal of a strong Turkish or Turanian state. This state was to be led by a single *Başbug* (Commander), who would serve as the head of the nation-army. This was the way the right made sense of and interpreted the Kemalist War of Independence. While the leftist opposition to the state gradually grew more radical, the radical right began to counter it with a defense of the *Turkish* state as the supreme authority and with a set of authentically Turkish moral values.

In the 1970s, these incompatible projects polarized not just the youth, but also the entire political system. The right-wing political parties were attracted to the nationalist ideas of the radical-right MHP (Nationalist Action Party), or at least saw in its militancy a springboard for marginalizing the left and monopolizing power. The former Kemalist CHP (Republican People's Party), which under the leadership of Bülent Ecevit had switched to a social-democratic orientation, sought to distinguish itself from the radical left. But it was obliged to take into account the left's aspirations for such things as "national independence" and "social justice" and to offer some space (at local branches) to radical left militants.

Although embraced and sanctified by two competing radical political liturgies, violence in Turkey during the 1960s and 1970s cannot be explained solely by ideological polarization. Once it started in 1968, violence opened the Pandora's box of Republican Turkey, revealing other sources of conflict in society that were already extant or were emerging as a consequence of rapid social changes. One can even say that the leftist and rightist radical discourses provided these infra-political conflicts with two alternative universal syntaxes and bases of legitimization. The rapid polarization of formerly peaceful provincial Anatolia also showed the degree to which the traditional mechanisms of conflict regulation had weakened or even ceased to exist.

Violence, or the Failure of Republican Unanimism

As observed above, Republican Turkey experienced very little violence during its first five decades. The reason for this was not, as many observers in today's Turkey nostalgically imagine, that the Turkish "nation-army" was unified around the Six Arrows[52] of the Kemalist revolution. On the contrary, the Republican unanimism that presented the society as a corps unified around these principles was accepted simply because it constituted the only authorized system of representation. As under most authoritarian regimes, the official unanimism was made obligatory not in order to achieve higher levels of mobilization, but only in order to secure the outward conformity that the official dogma required. The Kemalist concord did not mean the elimination of internal divisions or group interests. What made Republican Turkey relatively peaceful was that the main conflicts that emerged among social and community groups were often local and could be resolved, or at least regulated, by webs of local mechanisms of arbitration and submission. The state authorities, confined to their "new towns," were seldom involved in or even aware of these conflicts.

But as Şerif Mardin suggested years ago,[53] by the 1960s these traditional mechanisms of domination and arbitration ceased to be effective in Turkish society. The rapid pace of social changes did not allow for new autonomous mechanisms to replace them. For instance, the vendetta system had become largely defunct, and in the few places where it was kept alive it functioned more as a means of widening and aggravating conflicts and violence than as an institution regulating them. The consensual local boards that used to bring together the dignitaries or elders from the villages and provincial towns involved in a conflict had ceased to function. The influence of the religious brotherhoods, which in the past had provided mechanisms of arbitration, also weakened. Finally, unprecedented social mobility severely challenged the traditional social authority of elders as greater numbers of the young moved away from the local elders in the villages and provinces to the cities. Moreover, the youth were better educated than their elders. Thanks to their newfound knowledge and ambitions, they naturally challenged the existing hierarchical power relations.

The high social and political mobility exacerbated the consequences of the weakening of these traditional mechanisms of regulation and arbitration. During the Kemalist period, material resources were rather limited, and only some high-ranking civil servants, *affairistes* close to power, and a very frail bourgeoisie could access these resources. The symbolic resources were even scarcer, in the sense that the party-state dominated the political sphere. The Republican People's Party appointed the parliamentary deputies and imposed a single political discourse and a unified vision of the nation.

In contrast to the Kemalist period, the economic growth of the 1950s and 1960s, financed largely by foreign aid and investment, created new material resources and gave birth to new political programs. The political pluralism accepted in 1946 broke the former party-state credo in parts and presented a space for competitive symbolic systems. But to gain access to these resources one had both to challenge the well-established notable families in the provincial towns and to compete with other groups seeking to claim and monopolize the same material resources.

This competition was, above all, economic. But acquiring economic resources required group mobilization. Only more or less hierarchically organized groups could impose themselves at the provincial level and take part in patron-client relations. Access to economic resources was, therefore, pre-conditioned by access to political resources. The political resources themselves were symbolic ones. In a more and more competitive arena, politics could not be isolated from group identities, affiliations, and symbols. The competition required a move from the material field to the symbolic one.

To some extent, the inclusion of the symbolic field in the competition over resources was not an unexpected process. In his analysis of the violence of the 1970s, Şerif Mardin insisted on a dialectic relation between dissimulation and visibility in Ottoman, Kemalist and post-Kemalist Turkey. [54] By dissimulation he meant that in some conditions, social, ethnic, and sectarian groups could not openly contest the official unanimism and therefore could not express their differences. These groups thus tended either to hide themselves or to express their differences by violent contest. But when conditions permitted, the formerly hidden groups ceased to play this game of conformity and insisted on being visible and exposing their differences.

By the 1960s and 1970s, the official sources of unanimism, which had imposed conformity and dissimulation upon the entire society, ceased to be effective. As a consequence of the mass political mobilizations, the Kemalist civil religion no longer was accepted as the normative basis for the social order or as the official system of representation. The post-Kemalist regimes, recognizing that that project

69

had failed, nevertheless attempted to replace Kemalism with another legitimizing ground of authority—Islam—and founded their political order not on the Six Arrows but on three national goals previously articulated by Gökalp[55]: Turkification, Islamization, and Modernization.

But instead of creating a new unanimity, the establishment of Islam as an official source of political legitimacy gave birth to new social tensions. Not only did some sections of the military accuse the political authorities of betraying the Kemalist heritage of secularism, but the Alevis, a sectarian and mainly endogamous group comprising up to 20% of the population who were excluded from the Gökalpian and Kemalist versions of unanimism, were goaded to mobilize under a different banner. The Alevis felt obliged to proclaim, through poetry and music as well as popular meetings and marches, that Turkish society was far from being the simple and neatly homogenous "99% Muslim" society that the official ideology claimed. Moreover, the acceptance of Islam as an official source of legitimacy naturally strengthened the Islamists, whom the state traditionally had considered a threat to the Kemalist revolution. In a matter of years, the Islamist opposition succeeded in transforming itself from a loose collection of intellectuals into an organized mass movement. This new opposition did not reject "Westernization," as has so often been alleged, but it did reject the state's presumed right to intervene in the private or communal sphere. Some Sunnis, mainly those in the so-called mixed areas where they lived alongside the Alevis, adopted radical-right positions. The radical right not only hailed Islam as one of its fundaments, but also transformed it into a weapon against the left-wing Alevis. In fact, both the radical right movement and the most conservative Islamists considered Alevis to be alien to the Turkish nation and to Islam, and saw them as a fifth column of the communist and atheistic threat against Turkey.

By the 1970s Turkish society was deeply fragmented. And while the demands of the Kurds might have been satisfied by the expedient of geopolitical separation, other cultural and political groups could not be so simply reconciled. The Alevis and Sunnis shared common territories; Islamists and Westernizers found themselves side by side in the country's big cities, at the universities, or on the Bab-i Ali Avenue, the famous street lined with newsstands and bookstores in Istanbul. Thus, by the 1970s, it became ever more urgent to negotiate a contract that would permit the integration of these different groups and the identities that they claimed into the political system. This could have been possible had the state had ceased to insist on unanimism. The recognition of the autonomy of the various sectarian groups in the religious field could have pacified relations between the Alevis and Sunnis and de-politicized the Islamist opposition; indeed, acceptance of a degree of multiculturalism and a policy of de-centralization could even have satisfied the Kurdish nationalists.

The country's civil and military bureaucracy, however, failed to develop such a contract and the requisite mechanisms of integration. Instead, the Turkish-Sunni group, or rather the Turkish-Sunni-Westernized group, won the status of *asli kitle*—what we might call the dominant social entity—while Kurds, Alevis, Islamists, and others were defined as potential internal enemies. The (implicitly secularist) Turkish-Sunni-Westernized group, largely supported by the state, would accept neither a position of equality with the others, nor the construction of a public sphere wherein ethnic, sectarian, and political cleavages could be recognized. In response, the marginal groups re-

71

fused to play the game of dissimulation any longer, i.e., they refused to accept an inherently subordinate position. Instead they tried to assert their agendas through violence. The absence of a flexible social contract pushed each one of them in turn to try to monopolize the power at the only level they could: the provincial level. This power-monopolization required the use of violence and accelerated the fragmentation of Turkish society.

The extreme polarization of the society between left and right-wing movements—and, more worryingly, at the provincial level, between Alevis and Sunnis, Kurds and Turks—provided vivid proof of the failure of the Gökalpian and Kemalist unanimisms, which had aimed at the creation of a Turkish, Sunni by default, and in any case "Westernized" nation. But it also meant the failure of the alternative "counter-unanimisms," such as the leftist vision that espoused the concepts of anti-imperialism and of social revolution as the denominators of a future Turkey. The leaders of the leftist movement originated from all parts of Turkish society. Some of them were Sunnis, other Alevis, Kurds, Turks, or even Armenians. Some were from wealthy families. Others had poor rural or provincial origins. All of them, however, miscalculated the dynamics of the fragmentation of society. None of them could foresee, for instance, that the Sunni populations of the intermixed areas would move so sharply to the radical right or that the dominant political class and the civil and military establishments would find in these strata an important political resource. The establishments in turn failed to foresee that the dynamics of the growing radical right could enable it to acquire a political and military autonomy that the state could no longer keep under control.

The Repertoires of Violence

Shortly after the end of military rule in 1973, the country entered what the chronicles call the "period of violence." This period started with the assassinations of 1974 and continued until the military coup d'état of September 12, 1980.

Different repertoires of violence co-existed during these years. The clashing social projects and visions of the radical right and radical left generated violence among and between the student movements in Istanbul and the other major cities. The mobilizations of the working class and peasants for the pursuit of economic and social goals also produced some violence. But the main form of violence, that which made many observers believe that civil war was imminent, was the militia violence. The militias—often well-organized armed groups, based either on a communitarian affiliation or on a socialization circle, who exerted a strong military control over some suburbs or towns—adopted the broader left- and right-wing discourses, and militia violence was especially prevalent in the mixed, Alevi-Sunni and Kurdish-Turkish provinces and in the mixed districts of Istanbul, Ankara, and Izmir. Moreover, the perpetrators of this violence had organic ties to both the radical left and right organizations that were active in the rest of Turkey. Although they monopolized the material and symbolic resources in the areas under their control, the militias did not try to establish a new political system. Most of all, the militia phenomenon represented the "autonomization" of local actors through the use of the instruments of violence and the capture of municipalities and their resources. During this period, controlling a municipality in provinces such as Sivas, Maraş, or Erzurum, in fact, become even more important than holding the seat of deputy or senator in Ankara.[56]

Another kind of violence accompanied the militia violence. This was the intimate violence that pitted neighbors or different *hemşehri*[57] webs against each other. For example, in an act of indictment prepared in 1982 by a military prosecutor[58] in Ankara, 594 persons are accused of taking part in the activities of Dev-Yol, a left-wing organization. One hundred thirty-six of them originated from three provinces (Çorum, Sivas, and Yozgat). Many of the indicted persons had been involved in a socialization process built on the previous links of *hemşehrilik*. This "juridical" sample is heterogeneous, grouping together young and old people, people without education and people with university diplomas, unemployed people and engineers. The indicted persons were accused of 70 murders and 233 bombings. Although the available biographical information is far from satisfying, a brief analysis of a sample of the seventy victims of violence shows that only thirty-two of them were "ideological enemies" of the left (that is, militants of the radical right) or state agents. The others were simply neighbors. Similarly, only 18% of the bombings targeted either the radical right's associations and buildings or state interests, while almost 60% of the targets were neighboring houses. The attacks were markedly more frequent during the New Year season. This heightened frequency appears to be linked to the fact that during the festivities people tend to display their wealth more openly. "Ideology" in this instance seems to have offered a cover for an act of destruction that otherwise would have been ascribed to jealousy or economic inequity.

Fragmented Society, Fragmented Violence

This fragmentation among the ordinary people testified to how deeply the mechanisms of social cohesion and regulation had weakened in Turkey by the 1970s. But it also showed the incapability of the state to protect its citizens' lives or even to arbitrate their everyday conflicts. The state's authority within society was in fact significantly weakened. In many provinces, in fact, the only official representations of the state were army detachments whose influence was often confined to their own barracks. Moreover, like the police forces, the army itself was starting to reveal signs of fragmentation. Some army officers were almost openly linked to the radical right movements, while the others were affiliated with the moderate left-wing parties.

The violence of the 1970s demonstrated that violence, once started, could become a legitimized pattern of action. By becoming more and more linked to the infra-political levels, it reflected the gravity of the tensions and fragmentation within society and accelerated them in turn. This fragmentation was something quite different from the traditional division of Turkish society along communal lines. The process of fragmentation divided the communities themselves, thereby preventing the creation of more or less structured power blocks. The left-wing movement was divided into several groups, and some of them used violence against each other. At the national level, the radical right was more unified than the radical left, but this unity did not mean that decisions made at the center were accepted or implemented at the provincial or suburban levels. Moreover, discrete groupings also existed within the radical right and were often in competition with each other.

But the violence of this decade was important for two more reasons. First, a tragic vision of politics had seized the actors, especially after the 1977 elections, which put an end to the hope of a peaceful resolution to the violence.[59] In the minds of the radical left and right, a deadly conflict that could end only with the elimination of one of them was ineluctable. Their conception of time itself became cramped, in the sense that those involved in the violence could not contemplate their future in a long-term time frame. They could act only within the framework of day-to-day survival. Survival meant not just wielding weapons, but also shirking or escaping any moral and legal responsibility. This perspective led to the justification of all kinds of violence, including pogroms and massacres. For the civil and military bureaucracy, itself divided between the left- and right-wing factions, the phenomenon of violence also constituted a trauma, not least because it pointed to the possibility of the disintegration of the state itself. This tragic vision and this trauma, which, in turn, became a cause of violence, greatly influenced the evolution of Turkish politics in the following decades.

Second, violence gave birth to a new process of socialization. The youth was obviously the main element in this process. By 1980, many university students, and also young boys in high schools or even elementary schools, had their own socialization circles. The circles of the "elders," i.e. those who were over the age of fifteen, typically embraced some degree of violence. Radical commitment—or at the least a very fast politicization—marked the younger members.[60] Some of the circles formed in 1975 and 1976 appeared to possess a geographic reach that extended beyond the locality where they had been formed. The "friends" who built these circles moved to the large cities of Istanbul and Ankara, where they become leading figures of the radical-right movements.[61] These circles played a decisive role in the ascension of the young militants, but this ascension itself required new alliances and contacts with other kinds of networks. The "militants" used their *hemşehrilik* networks and mafia structures based, at least partly, on these same links. Already by 1979, the radical-right militants were acting as sub-contractors for "underground" bosses. Some of the radical-left movements seem also to have contracted alliances with the "leftist" or "Kurdist" bosses such as Behset Cantürk.

The older generations dominated the *hemşehrilik* and mafia networks. Those generations, in fact, simultaneously presented two different responses to the "violent" socialization of the young militants. The first was to declare a "moratorium"[62] that accepted the violent "autonomization" of the youth. This attitude, which prevailed throughout all the regions of all Turkey, was a fatalistic one. The older generations simply did not understand the crisis gripping the entire country. As in similar situations, violence was perceived as an anonymous and uncontrollable force that annihilated or erased social determinants such as power relations, socialization processes, or economic dependency.[63] Thus, they resigned themselves to the matter, expecting that when the youth matured the old hierarchical orders and the preeminence of the elders in the society would be re-established.

The second response was more cynical, and many dominant figures of the *hemşehrilik* and mafia networks, as well as many right-wing politicians, embraced it. It was the use of the dynamics of violence to pressure the left-wing movements, or the use of the younger generation as a "policing" force of sorts, a force that sometimes could be used to provide extra muscle to mafia groups.

The 1980 Military Coup

The 1980 coup (described by James Rule as Hobbesian[64] because it provided the army, the strongest power, with the legitimacy that it sought), put an end to this period of violence. It is true that the army employed severe means to stop the violent strife and paid little attention to individual human rights or to public liberties. But the army's swift victory also showed that the civil violence, despite its omnipresence, had a weak structural foundation. Under the stresses of military rule, community protection of young militants crumbled. Many families, in fact, who were already troubled by the rebelliousness of the youth, actually denounced their own children to the authorities because they thought that by imprisoning them for a couple of years, the military would at least protect their lives and allow them to mature. (In this they were cruelly mistaken: many militants were killed under torture or executed.)

But the peculiar genius of the army, and a key to its success, lay, paradoxically, in a strange species of tolerance. Although the new regime convicted and executed some radical-right militants, it co-opted many others and retooled them for its own ends, in part by emphasizing the similarity between the discourse of the radical right and that of the military. As revealed by the Susurluk scandal of 1996, which I will discuss below, the military offered many radical-right militants the chance to "keep silent" for a couple of years or to work "for the state" abroad. Many of those militants who had been allowed to leave Turkey were later integrated into the official security force structures.

Crisis as a Technique of Social Engineering and Social Fatigue: Turkey in the 1980s and 1990s

The analysis of the issue of violence in Turkey in the 1980s and 1990s requires a brief discussion of the political developments of these decades. The trauma of the violence of the 1970s and the disastrous heritage of the military regime led the political parties and public opinion to reject any radical program or coercive policy. The end of the 1980s and the turn of the 1990s represented a period of political stability during which many options seemed to be open, from achieving greater democratization and internal peace at home to accelerating integration into Europe and attaining a measure of real influence in Central Asia and the Balkans. Although the military ultimately determined the boundaries of politics, for the first time in the history of the Turkish Republic, the Kurdish issue, the Islamist movement, the Alevi question, and the nature of Kemalism could all be discussed openly. The Prime Minister and then President of the Republic from 1989 until his death in 1993, Turgut Özal, evolved during these years from a very conservative, right-wing politician into a genuine political reformer willing to resolve the Kurdish issue through administrative measures and through the integration of the Kurdish actors into the country's legitimate political life.

The period that began in the wake of the marginalization and subsequent death of Özal in 1993 can aptly be described as an era of "government as crisis management."[65] "Crisis" management in the Turkey of the 1990s meant branding the Kurdish movement and the Islamist opposition as "internal enemies" and assigning priority to state security imperatives to the detriment of democratic reforms. The crisis was used as an excuse for disciplining society and constructing an official state syntax based on Turkish nationalism and Kemalist secularism. This policy targeted moderate Kurdish and Islamist activists as well as the liberal thinkers who had been stigmatized as *liboş*[66] who had betrayed the country. This incessant process of discrediting advocates of political solutions for the country's major problems was part of the doctrine of "Low-Intensity Conflict" that the security forces had adopted at the beginning of the 1990s.[67] This doctrine weakened politicians who advocated liberal and pragmatic policies. With their weakening, the radical protagonists who had been defined as enemies lost "translators"[68] who could have built a bridge between them and the rest of the society and made possible their progressive integration.

As a result of this "politics as crisis management," Turkey throughout the 1990s was a theater of constant mobilizations and counter-mobilizations. The radicalization of the Kurds and the Islamists during this period went hand-in-hand with the mobilization and outbidding of the Turkish nationalists, Kemalist intelligentsia, and the military and civil establishments. The 1999 elections, the high point of these counter-mobilizations, successfully led to the formation of a coalition government bringing together the nationalists of the left and right.

But no society can afford permanent mobilizations. After the 1999 elections, the mobilization campaigns inevitably lost considerable strength. After years of tension, all sectors of Turkish society found themselves experiencing a crisis of meaning. They could not easily give a sense to Turkey's immediate past—a past full of crises calling for further sacrifice and blood, a past that could not inspire hope or trust in a foreseeable future. The severe economic crises of 1999 and of 2000–2002 transformed that "present" itself into an ordeal, with survival in the conditions of pauperization becoming the main concern of millions of people.

Although it managed to maintain its coercive power, the state itself now looked to be incapable of exploiting crisis as a technique for managing society. The weakening of the Kurdish guerrilla, the opposition Islamist, and the radical left-wing movements led to a massive mobilization of pro-state opinion and support. But the successful marginalization of these forces left no more social enemies. The designation of new enemies, such as the Islamist figure Fethullah Gülen who was identified as Turkey's new "Public Enemy Number One" in 2000, led to no massive mobilization. In fact, Gülen, who now has been labeled a terrorist for over two years, had always been a very pro-state and pro-nationalist figure who condemned opposition to the state. (He has since become much more tolerant towards the Kurdish, leftist, and Islamist oppositions as a result of the campaigns launched against him, but he continues to condemn all forms of radicalism.) In labeling such a man as a prime enemy, the state reveals that its rhetoric is merely situational, based only on its own immediate need to designate an enemy—any enemy—and not on any objective criterion of threat.

Hence at the end of the millennium and the beginning of the new one, social fatigue and wariness of official pronouncements replaced the condition of constant mobilization in Turkey. But this does not mean that Turkish society is more unified at the beginning of the third millennium. On the contrary, one can readily observe a profound segmentation between Kurds and Turks, Alevis and Sunnis, Islamists and Kemalists. Very metaphorically speaking, today's Turkey is divided between a broad *bled as-siba* (Kurds, Alevis, Islamists) and probably an equally broad *bled al-makhzen* (Kemalist Sunni Turks). As scholars of Morocco have put it, *as-siba* is the territory of dissidence, the opposite of the state-controlled *al-makhzen*. In the Turkish case, rather than territories of dissidence, one may speak of segments of dissidence that identify themselves neither with the state nor with any political party.[69]

This *siba* is not a zone of unified oppositions, but rather represents a further degree of social fragmentation. It is composed of multiple webs of non-state relations and informal networks that function as the only integrative social mechanisms. And although its fractured state prevents large-scale campaigns, this *siba* continues to produce violence.

State as "Primus inter Pares": The Issue of Violence in Turkey in the 1980s and 1990s

Aside from the PKK's guerrilla warfare and terror, violence ceased to be the central issue of Turkish political life after the 1980 military coup. But violence did not cease. It simply changed shape, becoming much more fragmented and multiform than before. It pitted not political and military forces but locally organized actors and the state or nationwide mafia-type networks against each other.

To some extent, the state itself changed both its perception of the violence and its techniques for dealing with it during these decades. Following the military coup of 1980, the Turkish state went through important changes both in its own organization and in its perception of society. It grew capable of integrating more and more social and political forces, from "loyal" Kurdish tribes to the left-Kemalist intelligentsia, directly into its political and security structures. As the sociologist Ümit Cizre argues, the political system during these decades, but especially during the 1990s, was transformed into a "cartel."[70] This cartel ceased to produce political programs and lost its capacity to represent the electorate, but it remained as a form of state-integrated parliamentary representation and as a resource-allocating mechanism for the political parties, their leading figures, and their members and client groups. As a consequence of these transformations, the state became a field of complex games of co-optation, competition, and resolution of conflicts.

The main result of this metamorphosis was that the state refused to assert its monopoly over the instruments and exercise of coercive violence. To the contrary, it accepted the principle that some degree of violence should and could be acceptable, but under one condition—that ultimately it remain under the state's control. The military authorities certainly knew that such a redistribution of the instruments of violence would deepen the social fragmentation of society, but they also understood that, in turn, it could enable the state to conduct an open game of contracting (and ending) alliances in a fragmented space.

This transition from the centralization of violence to decentralization was not unprecedented in Turkish history. By the end of the nineteenth century, for instance, Sultan Abdülhamid II successfully transformed some rebellious Kurdish tribes into the state's allies by creating a Kurdish *makhzen*. The tribes were used against the Armenians, but enrolling them in the state's service also deflected potentially anti-state energy into intratribal violence. The state acted in a similar way in the 1980s and 1990s when it formed the Corps of "Village Protectors." The aim of this tribal militia of nearly 100,000 men, armed and salaried by the state, was not so much to fight the PKK's guerrillas directly, but rather to constrain the PKK's room to maneuver and to deprive it of potential allies. The Village Protectors, in fact, very seldom engaged in combat. Rather, the tribal chiefs participating in the corps used the salaries and weapons generously accorded to them to strengthen their positions within their own tribes and to become state's "most favored lords." The policy led to a process of retribalization of the Kurdish areas—with the unintended effect that some tribes that could not profit from the state's resources tried to locate other resources by seeking alliances with the PKK.

But the policy of tolerating and integrating a fragmenting violence was not limited to intra-tribal issues. The state also armed Hizbullah, a non-tribal radical Islamist organization, against the Kurdish nationalists,[71] and may even have armed Sunni villagers against the Alevis in the 1990s.[72]

This policy created a complex web of patron-client-patron relations. The state was obviously the "patron" of the groups to which it distributed arms and salaries, but locally, in many cases, the tribes themselves become "patrons," clientizing the state's agents and insuring them with their protection. The state became a kind of "first among equals" on the field of violence, but one unable to control the dynamics of a process of violence that it had itself encouraged and authorized. For instance, in 2000, state authorities decided to end their alliance with Hizbullah, a group that in one decade had slain hundreds of intellectuals, including Islamist intellectuals who opposed it, and they killed Hizbullah's leader, Hüseyin Velioğlu. The response came the same year—Hizbullah assassinated the Chief of Police in Diyarbakir as well as half a dozen collaborators. The Village Protectors themselves threatened to change alliance if the state did not continue to support them financially and militarily. Kamil Atak, member of the radical right MHP (Nationalist Action Party), head of the Village Protectors, and Mayor of Cizre, put it clearly: "if the state abandons us, we will serve those who give us weapons."[73]

The Privatization of Violence

The second significant change in the field of violence during the 1980s and the 1990s took place within the state itself. As I mentioned earlier, many militants who had been in the ranks of the radical right during the 1970s succeeded in capitalizing upon their organizational ties to form a nationwide network of patron-client relations. In the 1990s many of them "reinvented" themselves as respectable businessmen or politicians. The 1999 elections in particular permitted many former militants, including those condemned for politically motivated acts of homicide in the 1970s, to become deputies.[74] Many others obtained important positions in the power structures in the provinces.

The successful reinvention of former radical militants transferred violence from the periphery of the state into its very heart. In fact, during the 1980s and 1990s many of those militants contracted alliances with mafia structures and the security forces, and were active in the underground economy. By the middle of the 1990s they were able to move with great ease between the circles they constructed during the 1970s, their underground political and business networks, and the intelligence agencies of which they were an institutional part.

These complex webs of affiliations were exposed when Abdullah Çatli, a known radical-right militant in the 1970s who had spent many years in prison in France and Switzerland for drug-trafficking and

who was sought for a dozen homicides, was killed in a car accident in
1996. Hüseyin Kocadağ, a high-ranking Istanbul police official, was
in the car with him and also perished in the accident. One passenger
survived: Sedat Bucak, the chief of a famous Kurdish tribe as well as
of a private army of ten thousand men. Bucak, who was very close to
Süleyman Demirel, Turkey's president, was himself a deputy of the
DYP (True Path Party) of former Prime Minister Tansu Çiller. The
investigations and parliamentarian inquests that were opened after the
accident did not unveil the web of relations behind this coalition in
their entirety. But they did reveal that the three men were a part of a
"uniformed gang," one of nine such gangs working within the state.
These gangs operated under the protection of higher authorities[75] and
took their share of the abundant resources created by the war in the
Kurdish regions and the international narcotics trade.

These gangs constituted a crossroads where politics, state coercion, and mafia-type violence mixed and melded. The emergence of
the gangs within the intelligence services and the security forces was
a direct consequence of the post-1980 policy renouncing the state's
monopoly on coercion in favor of legitimizing the employment of
violence by semi-autonomous non-state actors. But it was also a consequence of the transformation of the state itself.

As I have emphasized above, the state during the 1980s and the
1990s became a field of competition between different elected and
non-elected bodies. At the same time it possessed much more effective means of coercion than in the past, and a vigorous body called the
National Security Council that dominated state decision-making. But
the material and symbolic resources created by the state and its policy
in the Kurdish areas were simultaneously attractive and insufficient.
They were attractive not least because they offered official protection

to gang members and provided them with sophisticated weapons and official documents, including diplomatic passports. But they were insufficient because the main material resources and the channels to access them were tied to drug trafficking and the underground economy. The security forces, and especially the competitive intelligence agencies, which recruited widely among the radical-right militants, were thus compelled to establish unofficial patron-client relations with the mafia bosses.

The Mafia as a Conduit for Economic Mobility and Violence

Thousands of documents made available after the Susurluk incident attested[76] to the fact that political violence in Turkey was heavily linked to mafia activities. (By Mafia, one should understand a complex web including the underground economy, drug and weapon trafficking, as well as a widespread praxis of racketeering, requiring blacklisting and killings.) Although no systematic research has been done on the transformation of the mafia in Turkey,[77] the most reliable estimates suggest that the mafia links together some 45,000 people and handles financial resources ranging from 25 to 40 billion dollars a year. The mafia had been largely re-shaped during the 1980s, and in the 1990s it became an inescapable factor in political equations, making possible a switch from political or province-based militia violence to privatized forms of violence.

At first glance, the mafia activities may seem to be incompatible with the strong mechanisms of social control that one can observe in Turkey. In fact, in spite of a massive pauperization of sections of society from the 1970s to the end of 1990s, family structures continued to work efficiently during these decades.[78] Moreover, historically these structures were reinforced by the traditional conception of the home and of the streets as places of control and stratification. The street, the place of male visibility, has its own mechanisms of checks-and-balances, including an unofficial hierarchy and the preeminence accorded to the "elders"; no matter how collectively dominant men may be in Turkish society, as individuals they are often closely circumscribed.[79]

This social control makes the move to small-time criminality quite hard, if not impossible, in many cities and neighborhoods. Thus, in Turkey, as in many other Middle Eastern countries, the every-day criminality rate remains quite low in spite of a chronic economic crisis. The efficiency of these mechanisms of social control is certainly one factor preventing the emergence of the banalized violence that one can observe, for example, in Brazil. These same structures, however, largely prevent boys from the lower classes from gaining opportunities for individual emancipation and social mobility, and so exacerbate the underlying problems.

In the 1970s, participating in political or in the militia-style violence was one way to challenge the domination of the elders and to move from a hierarchical world controlled by fathers to another vertical organization wherein elder brothers reigned supreme.[80] As important as this hierarchical switch was the fact that the violence of the 1970s brought protection to the militants. It also offered them a counter-culture and new ideological discourses to legitimize their struggle. The elders were swiftly marginalized because they could neither understand the new discourses that legitimized their children's struggles nor propose alternative discourses, and their only option was to support a state-enforced moratorium.

Except in the Kurdish regions and some Alevi suburbs, the conditions of the 1980s and 1990s did not permit conflict to spread widely. The memories of the violence of the 1970s were still very fresh and the elders (and former militants) had learned a lot from their own experiences. They eased social control and allowed more freedom to the youth. For instance, even in more conservative milieus the youth could access the visible resources of the alternative "youth culture" such as pop music cassettes, T-shirts, and new-style cafés. However, sharing the external trappings of the youth culture did not mean that all were able to access the highly publicized but exorbitantly expensive material and symbolic resources available elsewhere in the country, such as sportswear and stereo equipment; nor were all youths able to participate in social activities like dating where it was considered immoral.

Joining the mafia structures thus became a way for young males to escape the mechanisms of family and social control, to drop out of sight, and to change social status. The mafia offered a comfortable, reproducible pattern. The profile of a typical mafia godfather in the tabloids demonstrated that a poor education was not an obstacle to access to material resources. On the contrary, when combined with courage and a willingness to use violence, mafia affiliation could bring much more than many years of education. Moreover, the predominance of the *hemşehrilik* links in the mafia networks brought at once both protection and a new sense of family. It allowed a young male to maintain the same initial circle of socialization he had constructed during his adolescence, but also to enlarge it to encompass much broader horizons.

Finally, being in the mafia structures offered greater comfort and legitimacy than did the violence of the 1970s. The violence of the

1970s meant daily risks. Risks were, of course, present in the mafia, and many mafia members were killed during the 1980s and the 1990s. But risk was not a constitutive element of daily life. Moreover, during the heavy economic crisis of the 1970s, people were obliged to share poverty. Families in rural areas and suburbs of big cities had to share their meager resources with the militants. During the 1980s and 1990s, the mafia changed the game. Joining the mafia meant gaining access to the rich resources that were available in the country, but not in the poor suburbs. It paid off for entire neighborhoods, and even beyond them. The mafia organization of Alaaddin Çakıcı, for instance, worked as a kind of central bank that engaged in large-scale resource allocation for the poor in many parts of Istanbul.

The change in social status made possible by joining the mafia went hand in hand with the building of new patron-client relations. These relations were mostly, but not exclusively, community-based. Ultimately, as the trajectories of dozens of former right-wing militants and the mafia bosses show, joining the mafia meant both constraint and opportunity. The constraints derived from competition with other mafia groups and to the need to find protection elsewhere from the political parties and security organs. The opportunities flowed from the ability to negotiate easily with the security forces and the political cartel, and, while conducting one's own private activities, to subcontract for them. Many of the mafia groups gained the chance to create symbolic alliances with the security officers, politicians, and, as a sign of peace, with the members of other mafia organizations.

One can thus easily understand why, in a country where small-time criminality is considered highly immoral, so many families and neighborhoods can praise mafia activities. Membership in the mafia is regarded as proof of bravery and social accomplishment. One can also readily see that many militants from the 1970s continued their activities within this new field, and that this field itself became a conduit of violence. Unlike the violence of the 1970s, this violence is not political. It is fragmented and privatized, and it serves mainly the interests of small groups. But it remains closely tied to politics through its links to political actors and the security forces.

The Fate of the Radical Left

I examined the Kurdish conflict in Turkey in the 1980s and the 1990s in chapter 1. It seems to me important to underscore here that the Alevi question also served as a significant source of violence in the 1980s and especially in the 1990s. Not only were the Alevis targeted as a religious community under the military regime of 1980–83, but also many Alevis were forced to move to the cities during the 1990s. As the massive destruction of the Alevi villages in the province of Sivas between 1992 and 1993 attests, this de-territorialization was not a consequence only of economic crisis or social mobility but also of an official state policy that since the 1960s had stigmatized the Alevis as "internal enemies." The massacres of 1993 in Sivas[81] and 1995 in Gazi[82] in Istanbul could also be interpreted as new pogroms targeting the Alevi community and constituting new links in a long history of persecution and martyrdom.

During the 1980s and the 1990s, the Alevis managed to create a specific, though non-territorial, political space. *Alevilik* ("Alevism") as a political and cultural concept emerged as a consequence of, or as a response to, the resurgence of the Kurdish and Islamist movements and the rise of a radical Turkish nationalism. Unlike those movements, however, *Alevilik* as a system suffered from a crisis of meaning. The Kurdish nationalist movement for decades had possessed a codified discourse and symbols, and could generate its own radicalization without being affected by the collapse of the socialist bloc. The Islamists espoused a universal discourse that could replace the universal utopic vision of the left wing, while the radical right-wing nationalists maintained their own discourse and symbols and presented themselves as the guardians of the state. The Alevis, in contrast, could neither seek shelter in a codified nationalist discourse nor adhere to Islamism or radical-right nationalism, and thus formulated a specific discourse, presenting their religious belief as the authentic and truly humanist philosophy of Anatolia.

During the 1960s and 1970s, the programs of the left wing had allowed the Alevis to legitimize their own particularism and claims within a universal discourse. But the legacy of the violence of the 1970s weakened the attraction of left-wing ideas during the 1980s, and the end of the socialist bloc and the transformations in China irreparably weakened the power of Marxist rhetoric. Last, but not least, the social-democratic movement led by Bülent Ecevit offered to many Alevis a space for integration and political representation in the 1970s. During the 1980s and 1990s, however, Turkey's official left parties also became parts of the political cartel, and therefore ceased to provide channels of integration for the Alevis.

The Alevis thus had two alternatives, and they took both of them. The first was to withdraw to a particularistic Alevi identity and legitimize Alevism as one part of the pluriculturalism of Turkish society. It is true that defining Alevism was not an easy task. Alevism, with its peculiar cosmology, could not be presented just as a sectarian community. The construction of the Alevi political syntax put the emphasis, paradoxically, either on the philosophical principles of this cosmology (namely tolerance and humanism) or on the universal character of Alevism as a rebellious and anti-despotic tradition. The second alternative was to enter the political field. Like the Kurdish and Islamist oppositions, the Alevis could also act as a part of *bled as-siba*. Alevis traditionally distrusted the state and the official political class. But whereas the Kurdish and Islamist movements were to some extent organized around political parties, the Alevis were not. In their case their largely informal networks replaced political parties.

The weakest of these networks are close to the state, while the mainstream networks are dominated by the left, and sometimes by radical left organizations such as Dev-Sol and TKP-ML.[83] These organizations, whose leading figures are in now their late 40s, have a long tradition of militancy and of mass organization. They constitute some of the very few cases in the world in which Marxist-Leninist (or Maoist) discourses of the 1970s were kept alive through the 1980s and 1990s without any major change. The inflexibility of these discourses is not surprising, in the sense that it allows these organizations to take the 1970s, the epoch of the martyrdom of their founding leaders, as a starting point. These discourses include hagiographies and a hermeneutic *da'wa*, i.e., a mystical ideology, totally inaccessible to outsiders, which is supposed to contain the key to understanding the past and unlocking the future. In fact, while appropriating some of the main symbols of Alevism, these left-wing groups give birth to a new kind of religiosity. One can easily compare their *da'wa* to the religious appeals of many groups who left Islam. While it offers a sectarian syntax, the "Marxism-Leninism" of these organizations ceases to be a simple ideology.

The history of these organizations consists of long lists of "martyrs." The founders, Mahir Çayan and İbrahim Kapyakkaya, were killed in 1972 and 1973 respectively. Since then, many hundreds of other militants have lost their lives. Both organizations have sacralized their founding generations and notions of martyrs and martyrdom. Dev-Sol built a cult of personality around its leader, Dursun Karataş, comparable to that of Abdullah Öcalan among the members and sympathizers of PKK.[84] While the early generations of leaders and militants, those who had been active during the 1970s, are apparently still in command, both organizations have succeeded in recruiting from among youth born in the 1970s or even in the early 1980s. These organizations, especially Dev-Sol, were heavily involved in the 1995 riots in the Gazi neighborhood of Istanbul, where they showed their capacity to constitute, in a crisis situation, a counter-authority structure.

The overall social fatigue that one observes in Turkey obviously limits the appeal and power of these organizations. This, however, does not mean the end of their activities. They continue to mount violent actions sporadically in parts of Anatolia where they have some guerrilla detachments (along the Black Sea coast and in the provinces of Sivas, Malatya, Maraş, and Tunceli). But except for the riots in Istanbul's Gazi district, this violence has failed to give birth to any mass mobilization, to create "liberated areas," or to change power relations in Turkey. Although they remain able to recruit new militants and thereby insure their institutional continuity, these organizations have failed to transform themselves into central actors of the Alevi movement[85] or to impose their *da'wa* as a collectively accepted cosmology.

As in the Kurdish case during the 1990s, this situation causes frustration and tension. The political blockages and the state's hostility forbid these organizations from moving towards pragmatism. As noted earlier, both organizations also sacralized their *da'wa*, and thereby transformed it into a non-negotiable absolute principle. Their discourses ceased to have any relation to reality, and the vision of unconditional revolution remains their minimum acceptable goal. The failure of Dev-Sol and TKP-ML to create a link between non-negotiable absolute principles and the political realities of modern Turkey accounts for their isolation even within the Alevi community.

The conditions necessary for popular mobilization and mass violence are thus missing. Violence therefore can be employed at most sporadically, either in an instrumental form (e.g. bank robbery, small-scale guerrilla attacks, etc.), or in the form of self-sacrifice. The attack of September 10 that I mentioned at the beginning of this chapter illustrates this switch from instrumental violence to self-sacrifice. As far as I know, this action was the only suicidal attack organized by a radical-left group in the country. But members of these organizations have on numerous occasions freely embraced other forms of self-sacrificial or self-directed violence, such as the death-fasts held by prisoners and by their sympathizers outside the prisons.

The Islanders: From Political Violence to Self-Sacrificial Forms of Violence

The death-fasts of 1996 resulted in the deaths of twelve militants. After a couple of months, the government of Necmeddin Erbakan finally agreed to negotiate with the fasters and accepted the mediation of left-wing intellectuals and human rights organizations. The transfer of the militants to the newly built F-type prisons, notable for their extreme and dehumanizing isolation, was stopped. Four years later, when the Ecevit government decided to transfer the militants to the F-type prisons, they began a new death-fast. This new fast proved to be more lethal. In December 2000, thirty-five militants died when the security forces intervened in the prisons. This operation, cynically called "return to life" by the government,[86] did not, however, lead to any popular mobilizations outside the prisons, not even in the Alevi neighborhoods as had been the case in 1996. But it did further radicalize the militants and their families. Since that time, more than a hundred prisoners have died, and two hundred thirty-five were released to obtain medical treatment (but many are condemned to lifelong paralysis).[87]

The government has accused Dev-Sol of ordering the death-fasts in order to increase the number of its martyrs. Although such a motivation certainly exists, it cannot explain why the militants continue to fast to their death and why they refuse all compromise. To answer this question, one must bear in the mind that prisons have a special significance in the *da'wa* and in the traditions of the radical left organizations.

Traditionally, the periods of military rule excepted, a clear-cut distinction between prisons and the outside world does not exist in Turkey. This rule also prevails for political prisoners. The frontier separating the two worlds is weak. Family relations and the socialization process continue between the internees and the externals. The prisons thus become a natural extension of what exists outside, including the radical organizations to which the militants belong.

The introduction of the modern F-type prisons, however, heralded the introduction of a real barrier that would break down this continuity, and create a vacuum of being and meaning for the militants. This vacuum means that the prisoner ceases to be a simple prisoner, i.e., a part of the society in spite of his status of internee, and becomes an "islander." Following the tradition of Mahir Çayan, who was killed in 1972,[88] Dev-Sol conceives of the prison as an island and the prisoners, particularly the martyred prisoners, as islanders.[89] Since communication with others is not possible when alone on an isolated island, being an islander means having severed communication with one's organization and with one's comrades. The island is an autarkic state in which the prisoner becomes the physical incarnation of an absolute principle. He or she alone is responsible for the integrity and the honor of the *da'wa*. The islanders are physically isolated, but each of them is, at the same time, a *terre de résistance* within a single common meaning and code of behavior that links the members to each other and to the organization. The prisoner is thus obliged to engage in a wholly mental, almost telepathic, communication with the other islanders. This communication is achieved by keeping alive the same voice and syntax and a steadfast absolutism.

No other metaphor than that of the islander (a metaphor constantly cultivated by Dev-Sol) could be more appropriate to describe the end of the mass political, social, and communal violence that had begun toward the end of 1960s in Turkey. But this metaphor reflects the replacement of the mass violence with a new, self-sacrificial form of violence that possesses an almost religious meaning.

CHAPTER THREE

From Instrumental
Violence to Self-
Sacrifice in the
Middle East

At the beginning of the 1990s, many observers predicted that, after the Latin American countries and the Eastern European bloc, the Middle East would give birth to a third wave of democratization in the world. More than a decade later, one must confess not only that authoritarian power structures in many Middle Eastern countries have grown stronger, but also that new waves of violence have shaken some of these countries. While Tunisia, Syria, and Lebanon have been pacified, the pacification came at the cost of institutionalized state coercion or foreign invasion. In Iraq, social violence and massive state coercion went hand-in-hand. Other countries such as Algeria and Egypt experienced intense civil strain and political violence. The violence in the former produced more than 100,000 victims, and nearly 2,500 in the latter. In the very atypical Palestinian case, violence diminished for almost a decade after the Oslo agreement before it took a more familiar but more brutal shape with the second Intifada. Finally, as the attacks of September 11 demonstrated, a de-territorialized violence bringing together citizens of different Middle Eastern and European countries emerged. In these latter cases, instrumental/rational and sacrificial forms of violence coexisted side by side.

The centrality of political violence in Middle Eastern politics in recent decades contrasts sharply with the generally pacific nature of everyday life in the region. In fact, compared to many Latin American and African countries, the crime rate remains quite low in the Middle East, with Algeria as probably the only exception.[90] But this absence of low-level violence is overshadowed by pervasive high-level political and civil violence.

Religion, Economy, History: Is There a Middle Eastern Exception?

Like most regions, what we call the Middle East is more a political and academic construct than a unified society, and it follows that violence in each subset of Middle Eastern society should be analyzed in light of the particular history and mindset of the people involved. It is obvious, for instance, that the same reasons cannot explain violence in Algeria and in Palestine/Israel, and that the politics of violence in Lebanon and Iraq differ. Still, as in other regions of human geography, the societies of the Middle East do share enough commonalities to legitimize their "construction" as a region. Not only did these societies share a common history for centuries, but they also exhibit similar anthropological patterns in their family and/or tribal structures and social hierarchies. In spite of the differences between the Middle Eastern regimes, they possess similar power structures with non-elected bodies dominant in the political space (*rais*, clergy, army, monarchy, etc.). Islam is a common religion that constitutes a key element in all the Middle Eastern societies except Israel, and all of them have experienced some form of politicized Islam during the last two decades. Finally, some issues concern all the societies of the Middle East. The Iraqi and Palestinian issues, for instance, impinge on all the societies of the region. The latter constitutes a heavy mortgage on the development of all the Middle Eastern countries, non-Arab Turkey and Iran included.

During the past two decades scholars have been debating the question of the cultural and religious exceptionalism of the Middle East, particularly with regard to the issues of both democracy and violence. Islam, which is often presented as intrinsically different from the two other monotheistic religions, and the "Middle Eastern culture," which is described as patriarchal in essence, are presented as the foundation of the Middle Eastern exception, forbidding any evolution towards democracy and a political order based on a social contract. After the attacks of September 11, some intellectuals and analysts and many politicians enthusiastically cited the hypothesis of this cultural/religious exceptionalism. The fact that the dominant perpetrators of violence in the 1980s and the 1990s legitimized their action with religious references, most notably the imperative of *jihad*, has been presented as the ultimate proof of this exceptionalism. It seems to me important to briefly examine this issue, not least because it determines the very terms of the debate on the violence in the Middle East.

It is obvious that *jihad*, one of the religious obligations that a Muslim has to fulfill, occupies a central place in the Muslim theory of the state and politics.[91] It can also easily be used to legitimize violence in the political sphere. Moreover, as too many examples of the twentieth century attest, *jihad* can also serve as a central element in non-religious rebellions against colonial powers or central states. But Middle Eastern societies cannot be reduced solely to their religious dimension any more than can other societies. As Maxime Rodinson suggested years ago, while the religion disposes a certain degree of autonomy and constitutes a central element in the Muslim imagination, it remains a political instrument that serves broader political goals and pawns.[92]

Moreover, there are many competing and clashing interpretations of *jihad*. Both Sunni and Shi'i religious authorities have used it to facilitate the legitimization of non-religious power structures. As Alfred Morabia noted, after the first waves of Muslim conquests, *jihad* became an instrument used to impose state authority and to justify internal coercion, rather than to legitimize external wars.[93] Furthermore, before becoming arenas of mass or individualized forms of violence in the second half of the twentieth century, most Middle Eastern societies were in fact rather pacific. Almost no political actor used either *jihad* or another religious concept to legitimize violence against Muslim rulers.

Likewise, economic explanations of Middle Eastern exceptionalism (including violence) strike me as implausible. It is true that the Middle East's relative economic underdevelopment gives birth to frustrations and creates a cost-benefit calculus that can make the risks of engaging in violence "rational" for gaining access to material resources. Pauperization has certainly led to sporadic riots and the growth of the informal economy, which often includes some degree of violence, in Jordan, Egypt, Morocco, and Tunisia. But neither pauperization nor informal economy can give rise to organized civil or political violence. Moreover, if in Algeria the violent militants come primarily from very modest social origins, that is not the case in Egypt, where the members of Gama'a al-Islamiyya are predominantly former university students. The militants conducting self-sacrificial forms of violence in Palestine generally enjoy a relatively high socio-economic status.[94] As a quick prosopographic overview of the al-Qaida members involved in the September 11 attacks or in the higher levels of the organization also attests, they represent a radicalism of riches and not that of the poorest Arabs.

Finally, resorting to historical patterns to explain Middle Eastern exceptionalism does not allow us to make much progress. In fact, as I will argue later, the forms of violence that we have been observing for the past few decades in the Middle East have little to do with those that existed prior to the nineteenth century. Nor are these contemporary forms of violence exclusive to the Middle East. One can observe instances of guerrilla warfare, institutionalized violence, and religiously legitimated violent struggles and even suicide attacks elsewhere in the world. One can, for instance, compare the situation in Algeria, where violence is at once institutionalized, fragmented, and very closely bound up with the political and economic spheres, to the situation in Colombia, where *violencia* has for decades been a part of a complex web of economic, political, and symbolic transactions. The suicide attacks of the Palestinian "martyrs" resemble in many important ways those organized by the Tamil Tigers in Sri Lanka. The sectarian violence that we observe in countries such as Iran and Pakistan (between the Shi'is and Sunnis), in Turkey (between Alevis and Sunnis), or in Lebanon, has equivalents in Christian countries such as Ireland, or in India.

The question of violence in the Middle East needs therefore to be reformulated: what factors produce violence in this region, and why are the mechanisms that should regulate it so weak? The answer to these questions is to be sought not in culture, religion, or history, but rather in politics and in the nature and structure of power relations.

Traditional Mechanisms for Regulating Violence

Although, as I contend, reference to history cannot support the hypothesis of Middle Eastern exceptionalism, it nonetheless assists one in understanding the emergence of and change in forms of violence in this part of the world. The historical sociology suggests to us that, just as in many European countries,[95] there existed local mechanisms in the countries of the Middle East for the control and regulation of violence. The mere existence of such mechanisms, of course, did not mean the absence of sporadic mass civil violence or massive state coercion. A few historical cases (such as the outbreak and repression of the Celalî Rebellions during almost the entire sixteenth century in Ottoman Anatolia) show that those mechanisms were, in fact, often fragile. These rebellions and the many smaller uprisings testify that pre-modern societies were also dynamic ones that produced conflicts that could not always be resolved by the existing mechanisms of domination and arbitration. Finally, the brutal repression of these rebellions may suggest that, in moments of serious crisis, power in the Middle East rests on coercion and not arbitration or the usual mechanisms of domination. These forms of mass violence and naked coercion, however, seem to be exceptions rather than the rule.

In his work on center-periphery relations in the Ottoman Empire, Şerif Mardin suggests a useful model for understanding the logic of these mechanisms and the sources of their strength and fragility.[96] According to Mardin, the center-periphery division was not a geographic, economic, religious, or ethnic one. The "Center" was composed of the Ottoman dynasty, the ruling elite of the civil and military bureaucracy, the high-ranking ulema, etc. The sultan's subjects at large constituted

106

the periphery. This periphery included the non-Muslim populations, who had an inferior juridical status, as well as the vast majority of Muslims. The periphery was organized into provincial entities, state-like entities with a derivative administrative status, *millets* or communities organized according to faith (including the Alevis, Yezidis, and Druzes), tribal units, and others. For the Palace, the most important imperative was to have interlocutors, a vast stratum of "most favored lords" who represented the communities of which they were recognized authorities. The main interest of the periphery, in turn, was naturally to restrain and limit the intervention of the center in its everyday affairs.

The main structural inequalities of the imperial structures were reproduced on the peripheral level. The peripheries were in fact organized on the basis of a complex system of domination and subordination among their multiple strata, whose own internal structures were often very hierarchical. These strata had locally negotiated domestic forms or codes of civility and responsibility that made communication and co-existence possible. These forms included mechanisms of conflict regulation. More comparative research is necessary to understand how these mechanisms effectively functioned. One observes, however, that, in some parts of the Middle East, the vendetta was one of these mechanisms and served to regulate violence. Among some communities, such as the Alevis, internal tribunals did exist (in some Alevi communities, they continue to work). Ivo Andric's masterwork, *The Bridge over the River Drina*, offers rich details of intercommunal (Muslim, Orthodox, Catholic) cooperation to preserve the autonomy of the Balkan provinces. Finally, in many parts of the Middle East, the tribal structures worked as integrative mechanisms. If they did not stop violence, they nonetheless contributed to the regulation of violence. While codifying the vendetta, they also allowed the establishment of non-violent modes of communication.

Violence was limited not because the model described above was ideal, or constituted a voluntary social contract. The pre-modern Middle Eastern societies, simply by virtue of being pre-modern, possessed limited resources for mobilization. They sought stability as a priority and required a non-written code to map their everyday relations and resolve "cheaply" their various conflicts. Violence, in fact, signified a costly enterprise, in both material and social terms, that the societies could not afford. The weakly centralized and bureaucratized pre-modern states were also compelled to support these violence-regulating mechanisms because the resources at their disposal were also relatively scarce. These states did not work as *fabriques de citoyens* and could not support or maintain an expansive centralized bureaucracy and a coercive force. They aimed at most to establish a general security and insure the collection of taxes. The state found that it could more easily achieve these limited aims by supporting the establishment of a category of "most favored lords" made up of interlocutors and representatives of different peripheral components. While interested in the increase of their wealth, these components lacked resources to support the rise of alternative centralized organizations.

The New Social Engineering and the Weakening of Traditional Solidarities

The phenomenon of violence that we have observed in the Middle East since the beginning of the twentieth century is, at least partly, a consequence of the destruction of these mechanisms of arbitration and regulation of violence. Since the first part of the nineteenth century, in fact, these structures have been progressively replaced, both in the Ottoman Empire and in Iran, by the institutions of the centralizing states. The process of centralization continued after the dissolution of the Ottoman Empire.

The centralization policy has universally been a rather successful one and, in the long term, has bolstered the states. It was, and still is, understood by the states' authorities as an imperative of state security. These authorities equate centralization in large measure with an increase in their coercive power. And the states have long wielded physical and symbolic coercion with efficiency in ways ranging from simple indictment to mass killings as in Iraq or in Syria.

But it was evident from the very beginning that coercion would not offer more legitimacy to the states. Even in the important provincial towns, in fact, the states' presence was often physically limited to the new administrative headquarters, constructed outside the old cities. The states' civil servants had only very weak links with the ruling local elites, and virtually none with the populace. Once they left the capital, the states' officers were in a "foreign country" where they faced "a long tradition of hostility."[97] Following the French model, the government servants stayed only a short time in their new locations, and were routinely rotated to different locations.

The central states were thus obliged to reinforce their presence outside the capital by adopting a selective policy of resource allocation and continually renewing a "stock" of allies. Although minoritarian and tribal dynamics on the one hand presented a permanent source of threats to the states, they also afforded the states abundant possibilities to exploit the tactic of co-optation. This was systematically the case in the rural areas, where, each time, the logic of *siba* (territory of dissidence) in the peripheries was counter-balanced by the possibility of constructing a *makhzen* (state-controlled territory). But the situation was not always that different in the urban areas, where the state had to mobilize different kinds of resource allocation mechanisms or was obliged to tolerate the existence of the informal "client" networks. Together with coercion, the policy of direct or indirect resource allocation allowed the states to face down social unrest, marginalize oppositions, and insure their own durability. The policy of centralization thus did not mean simply the implementation of a central bureaucracy; it also signified complex social engineering.

During the first decades of the twentieth century, this new engineering still coexisted with the old local mechanisms of domination and arbitration. The older mechanisms survived in the rural areas and at the provincial level. But they became largely obsolete by the second half of the twentieth century for two reasons. First, during these decades coercion in many Middle Eastern states had become a "doctrinal" imperative, the use of force being more and more justified by the official state ideology. I will comment later on this issue. Suffice it to say here that the "revolutionary" regimes in the Middle East in the second half of the twentieth century were able to wield coercion on a scale greater than could any regime before them. As Samir al-Khalil and Michel Suerat have demonstrated, in Iraq and in Syria state coercion did not aim solely at the elimination of the elite of the *anciens régimes*. These revolutionary regimes also sought maximum visibility in order to intimidate their citizens and destroy any collective social solidarity among them.[98] Elsewhere, in Turkey, Egypt, Algeria, and Tunisia, the coercion was not as massive and did not strive for such visibility, but it was institutionalized and regular and aimed to impose an official unanimism.[99] These new forms of coercion have largely destroyed the old social solidarities, as well as the old bonds of trust that had formed the base of the traditional mechanisms of arbitration and domination.

The second reason the old mechanisms became outmoded was economic and sociological: social mobility. During the second half of the twentieth century, all Middle Eastern societies experienced a massive rural exodus and jump in urbanization. The peripheries declined while two or three big cities expanded enormously. This wave of urbanization directly impacted the very nature of political movements and violence in Middle Eastern societies.

The Urban Demands

Traditionally, as Ibn Khaldun presciently observed in the fourteenth century, Middle Eastern rulers feared the rural areas and their centrifugal dynamics. Although urban centers did on occasion become arenas of struggle and resistance before the twentieth century, outside of such rare moments they were securely controlled either by the ruler himself or by the local dynasties. In contrast, in the Middle East in the second half of the twentieth century, while the countryside was still neither uniformly pacified nor under the state's control, it had nonetheless lost its political weight. The countryside no longer possesses the necessary resources and means to challenge the center, and seldom even attracts the media's attention. Urban movements, however, can potentially involve half or more of the population in all the countries of the Middle East, and therefore pose a much greater threat, not least because they can mount a struggle within the very center of power, in an area opened to the wider world.[100]

The cities thus become the arena where the state's legitimacy is negotiated, accepted or rejected. While survival remains always the primary and, if ultimately necessary, exclusive objective of a regime, the durability of a regime is not synonymous with its legitimacy. The state must constantly re-negotiate it and co-opt new segments. The real problem, however, is that urbanization—a process of the weakening of primordial affiliations, the formation of new social categories (youth, middle class, working class, intelligentsia, etc.), and the emergence of subjects in the sociological sense of the word—creates new dynamics and new demands that the state can neither easily satisfy nor master. The politics of resource allocation to some segments of urban populations can reduce the impact of these demands, but it cannot completely eradicate them.

The most important of these demands is the enlargement of the political spaces that the rulers and their unanimist vision of politics formerly dominated. It is true that political oppositions in the modern Middle East have taken different forms over the decades (Arab nationalism, left-wing movements, Islamism, etc.), and many of these attempted to counter the state's official unanimism with a unanimism of their own. But the main political demand throughout these decades has always been the integration of new urban social categories into political systems and the negotiation of a social contract that would end the preeminence of the dominant non-elected bodies. Middle Eastern regimes, even the most open ones, such as the Egyptian and Turkish regimes, have, however, preferred to deal with these oppositions as if they were simply the products of the conspiracies of external and internal enemies. The regimes justified the existing political structures as the principal warrants of social peace and cohesion. The quasi-monarchical republics, the system of *rais*, the domination by the military, the absence of political representation, and the reign of gerontocracy have always been presented as the price to pay for stability and order. Constraint and coercion often went hand in hand with a symbolic violence that stigmatized those who demanded the enlargement of the political sphere.

From Political Demands to Violence: Rationality and Perceptions

In almost all the countries of the Middle East, the ruling powers have exploited political blockages and crises as means to reject demands for enlargement of the political space and for negotiation of a new social contract. These political blockages and crises have not been just the consequences of external or internal constraints. They have also served as material and symbolic resources at the disposal of the ruling powers. As I explained in the second chapter in reference to the case of Turkey, they allowed the rulers to ensure their own durability. But this durability had a price: it drove many political actors to the conviction that no change could be obtained without violence or without overcoming the blockage by breaking it down. This perception of the futility of all forms of politics other than violent ones has been widespread in particular among the youth in the Middle East. And in all the Middle Eastern cases that I am aware of, the youth, in fact, have been, at least in the beginning, at the head of all violent struggles.

One could readily object that, in some cases, such as those of Algeria, Egypt, or Turkey, the conviction that no change was possible without violence was a purely subjective one. In fact, I would agree that, whatever their political affiliations might have been, the opponents of the Algerian, Egyptian, and Turkish regimes gravely misjudged the situation in their own countries. And by sacralizing violence, they closed the existing (albeit very thin) channels that could have led to their peaceful integration and, in the long run, to political changes. They also handed to the states the opportunity to expand their coercive policies, espouse a hegemonic discourse based on the notions of social peace and security, and find many alliances within the society, especially among the middle classes. The use of violence by some actors also limited the maneuvering room of the other political opponents, since the principle of security, already acknowledged as an imperative, provided a convenient tool to the state authorities for designating virtually all of the state's opponents as internal "enemies."

The actors who opted for violence also badly miscalculated both their own strength and the states' coercive capabilities. In many cases, violent opposition did not begin in response to the states' application of maximal coercion. More importantly, the opposition groups failed to consider the states' ability to counter violent opposition movements by marshaling greater resources for coercion. Instead, they committed the common but elementary error of assessing their prospects *in situ*, i.e., at the very moment they decided to move towards violent forms of action, without considering how a violent campaign would fare should the state choose to react with massive repression. As the destruction of Hama in Syria in 1982, the repression of the Shi'i rebellion in Iraq in 1991, or even the massacres attributed to the Algerian army all demonstrated, states can readily and disproportionately increase their coercive capabilities. A violent struggle always involves uncertainty. The basic assumption underlying such a struggle is that, with the passage of time, the struggle will find more and more supporters and fighters, and the state will be less and less capable of mobilizing its coercive capacities. Often, however, that is not the case. While the strength and abilities of the violent opposition remain, at best, unchanged, the state can almost always increase its coercive capabilities, sometimes seemingly without limit. In only one case, that of the Iranian revolution, the state proved unable to boost its coercive capabilities relentlessly. In the face of the increasing popular support for the revolution (but not necessarily for the violent struggle) the Iranian state's coercive apparatus, although as effective as ever, proved to be incapable of dealing with the new, mass challenge to the Shah's regime. The force of the Iranian revolution, as in any other revolution, however, has to be sought in its spontaneous, unorganized nature.[101] In all the other cases in the Middle East, violent opposition movements have proved unable to expand and increase their capabilities on a scale commensurate with the states' capabilities.

It is, however, important to add that violence, including the forms of violence labeled "instrumental" or "rational," can seldom be reduced to an entirely rational or calculated strategy. It starts either as a consequence of a subjective calculation of power relations, or, more often, as a result of the impossibility to continue to accept a dominant system of representation. In fact, as Michel de Certeau contends, violence is often directly linked to subjective impressions, notably to the impression that the dominant system of representation and its symbols, mottoes, and categories are neither normal nor self-evident. They become more and more "incredible" for many, who can no longer accept them. Violence thus tends to instigate or even impose a new collective political vocabulary. This vocabulary includes new words whose shared meanings are, subjectively at least, accepted as "meaningful" and "credible."[102]

It is, therefore, exceptionally important to keep in mind that a violent opposition's calculation of costs and benefits is closely linked to its own, peculiar perception of the "credibility" and "incredibility" of hegemonic meanings. The actors who employ violence in the Middle East have typically perceived themselves as the "announcers" of the credibility of the counter-meanings in which they believed. Often, they succeeded in demonstrating that the old meanings were, indeed, "incredible" and that the Emperor truly had no clothes on.

But their main postulate—that once the "people" recognized that the dominant meaning was simply incredible, they, or at least the "believers" among them, would reject it—was wrong. Trapped by an all-too-rational calculus based on false assumptions, and not by *irrationality*, they could not foresee that neither the "people" nor the "believers" constitute a sociological category. Nor could they anticipate that one could reject a dominant system of representation and yet still find means of accommodation with it. Moreover, rejection of the dominant system of representation did not necessarily mean the acceptance of the counter-unanimism promoted by the actors of violence. Finally, the actors of violence failed to recognize that dominant systems of representation were rarely wholly rigid ones. While holding on to their hard-core symbols (e.g. nationalism, cult of personality, glorification of founding revolutions or victories), the dominant Middle Eastern systems of representation proved to be quite flexible. Without great difficulty they expanded their repertoires to include the themes (e.g. religious references, notions of "national independence," etc.) and rituals (praying in mosque, religious programs, etc.) of the movements they combated. The integration of some elements of the new, "credible" meaning of the violent opposition into the state's own language led to the banalization of these elements. Thus, they ceased to be elements that referred to and defined only the perpetrators of violence.

Violence and Political Culture, Old and New

Another common explanation for the violence of the Middle East is the notion of "political culture." Obviously, some patterns of the past political culture are kept alive in the social and political imaginations of today's Middle Eastern societies. But these patterns have combined with a new framework that came to light only in the twentieth century. The notion of *mulk* (i.e. state as property) constitutes the main link between these old patterns and the new framework. In the old Middle Eastern (and in many non–Middle Eastern) political cultures, in fact, a victorious use of violence is always *post facto* legitimized as one of the constitutive elements of the *mulk*, i.e., the state itself. The word *dawla*, which connotes a change of fortune, conforms to the conception of the state as *mulk*.[103]

This conception of power is obviously not relevant for some Middle Eastern countries. For instance, in Algeria, Turkey, and Iran, the army or religious figures hold or ultimately control the reins of power. These non-elected bodies function as tightly closed power cartels. Elsewhere in the Middle East, however, the conception of the state as *mulk* helps us to understand both the power relations and the radical change in the logic of violence. Syria and Iraq (before the last war) were significant cases in this regard. In both countries, Pan-Arabism served as the legitimizing program of the single-party regimes. But in a short period of time, minority sectarian communities, the Alawites in Syria and the Sunnis in Iraq, managed to monopolize power. In a third phase, while the sectarian communities kept their privileged status, power transferred from these regimes to the families of al-Assad and Hussein. The final phase of this process of transferal led to the

117

marginalization of the brothers of Hafez al-Assad and Saddam Hussein and to the ascension of their sons. In Libya, Iraqi Kurdistan, and Tunisia—places where power is seen as a *mulk*—the monarchic option remains a possibility in the future. This evolution from republics to kingdoms makes monarchy an ordinary form of political rule in the Middle East.[104] But it also marks a transition from state coercion to a new form of privatized violence. The "state" coercion becomes in reality coercion exerted by the ruling families or on their behalf.

While powerfully influencing the nature of many states in the Middle East, this old political culture contains many concrete attributes that the challengers of the current rulers can contest by simple imitation. But other elements can also lead to direct challenges against the actual rulers. In fact, if the contemporary *malik*, or ruler, accepts the idea that power is his or his family's personal property, he rejects another constitutive element of the classical political theory of the Middle East: the notion of *adala*.[105] The absence of *adala*, the justice or fairness that rulers owe both to individuals and collectivities, transforms the ruler in the contemporary Middle East into a usurper. Finally, as the classical Ottoman example illustrates, the traditional *malik* had limited sovereignty. Although in some situations he could exercise his personal authority to take or spare the lives of his subjects, those situations were quite rare. In the vast majority of instances he had to work within the limits circumscribed by the Ottoman state's internal checks and balances. In the contemporary Middle East, however, these mechanisms are, to say the least, much weaker, having been destroyed for the sake of greater coercion as part of the processes of political modernization and centralization.

Thus, while invoking the Middle East's past political culture may help us to better understand power relations in the Middle East, it does not take us very far with the issue of violence. The reason for this is that violence, as both instrument and action, is praised in the startlingly new political culture of the twentieth century, a culture which can imagine neither separate political and social spheres nor power relations within the framework of a social contract, and owes very little to the Middle East's past. One can even contend that it emerged as a reaction to the old political culture, which, while being heavily autocratic, still sought consensus through a complex set of mechanisms of subordination and resource allocation, and paid at least some attention to the notion of justice, as it was established by a long tradition.

The new Middle Eastern political culture draws its origins from the debates between the intellectual circles of the Young Turk opposition. While appearing ultimately as very conservative and state-minded activists, the Young Turk circles, like revolutionaries elsewhere in Europe and especially the Russian Empire, glorified violence, assassination as a program, and the "blood feast" *per se*, without necessarily putting them into any kind of political/philosophical equation.[106] The Kemalist revolution in Turkey also praised, at least rhetorically, "violence" as one of its constitutive elements.[107] In the second part of the twentieth century, no matter what ideologies the regimes have advocated (secularism, nationalism, Islamism), violence has been conceived as *naturally* legitimate and therefore normal and unquestionable. In the conception that the founder of the Ba'ath Party, Michel Aflaq, had of politics, war was "the broadest, most complete, and most adequate field allowing for the blooming of our gifts, capacities, and heroism."[108]

As the founding act of authority, violence is, in fact, largely sacralized by the states. Almost all the Middle Eastern regimes legitimize themselves by referring to a hallowed moment of violence, be it a war of independence, a bloody military coup d'état, the execution of opponents, or revolution. As such, the original violence that made possible the founding of the regime is constantly reproduced by official discourses and ceremonials. War is celebrated as the beginning of a new man, * while enmity, i.e. mortal antagonism between "us" and "them," between "friends" and "foes," is considered the very basis of the official political philosophy. As Kenan Makiya has shown, all state-sponsored art in Ba'athist Iraq was devoted to representing and legitimizing this philosophy and the coercion it advocated.[109] The Iraqi case is not, however, a grotesque exception. Official art in Kemalist and post-Kemalist Turkey, which has been influenced by the model of Nazi Germany, is not all that different.[110]

The glorification of founding violence has been a constitutive element of mass education in all the Middle Eastern countries. Textbooks represent violence as almost naturally virtuous, requiring no further ethical anxiety or philosophical/ethical legitimization. Ultimately, the question of the legitimacy of violence is posed only in terms of its success or its failure. As Benjamin Stora has observed about the second Algerian war, "one can not teach with impunity that the principle of armed struggle is central in the edification of the nation, and be (at the same time) surprised that this is reprised in reality."[111]

This centrality of the theme of violence does not explain the concrete configurations in which violence emerges. But it makes clear that, while challenging the states, the perpetrators of violence actually reproduced the monolithic political culture of the states. Against the state's unanimism they opposed a new unanimism that could lead only to a new monopolization of the political space. Opposing the cartel of power—clergy, army, or the presidency—means, too often, a willingness to replace it with a new cartel. Opposing the domination of a

120

sectarian group in the state means, too often, a willingness to replace it with another sectarian community. While challenging the states, none of the violent opposition movements in the Middle East have been able to proceed to a change in paradigms and in programs.

The Quest for Unity and Victimization

A third element that explains the violence is found in the interpretation that Middle Eastern societies frequently assign to their past. In short, the past is seen as a succession of Western plots aiming to divide and weaken the Middle East.[112]

The Middle East is indeed fragmented into many entities. Very few of these states possessed an extended existence in the past as distinct political or administrative entities. Created in the wake of the Sykes-Picot agreements, almost none of them had a homogeneous population, and the borders of many divided not only the Arabs as a "nation," but also ethnic and sectarian communities, families, solidarity groups, and religious brotherhoods. During the decades that followed their creation, these states succeeded in insuring their own continued existence and constitute, henceforth, the primary frameworks for distinct cultural, political, social, and economic fields. They have irrefutably become decisive landmarks in the formation of individual and collective identities.

At the same time, however, the Middle East, and particularly the Arab Middle East, kept alive the ideal of unity throughout the twentieth century. One should note that this ideal was weakly rooted before the First World War. This weakness is itself one of the factors that explain the division of the region. With the exception of Israel,

the Middle Eastern map has been determined not only by the decisions of the European powers and/or the United Nations, but also by
the competitive, complex power games played by European patrons
and their Middle Eastern clients. Finally, the quest for unity did not
result in the creation of a unified Arab state. It failed not because the
European powers or America were opposed to it, but because the centrifugal dynamics in the Middle East were too strong. But this quest
nonetheless did give birth to a symbolic unity. The idea of being part
of a larger entity, and of having been divided by external powers, is
one that many intellectuals share not only in the Arab world, but also
in Turkey and Iran.

Two other elements reinforced this symbolic solidarity. One is
the Palestinian issue, which the Arabs generally interpret as a will-
ful constant humiliation of them, and as a deliberate Euro-American
plot to deprive one group of the Arabs, and therefore the Arabs as a
geopolitical whole, of a piece of their territory. Israel's policies, which
except for the interlude between the Oslo agreements and the second
Intifada explicitly and unyieldingly sought to deny any possibility of
a Palestinian state and to deprive the Palestinians of any hopes for a
state of their own,[113] constantly sought the humiliation of the Palestinians rather than a true reconciliation with them. The official Israeli
preference for force over negotiation could only aggravate this feeling
of humiliation and despair.

The second element is linked to the ideal of the solidarity of the
larger Muslim "nation," the *ummah*. Against the backdrop of this ideal, the history of Western interventions in the Muslim world, and the
Palestinian issue in particular, are perceived as only the most recent
campaigns in a broader and centuries-old Holy War waged by Christi-
anity and Judaism against Islam.

One can object that this interpretation of modern Middle Eastern history is mistaken and that it neglects or overlooks regional, internal, and domestic dynamics,[114] and can add that the mechanisms of exclusion and domination of the Armenian, Jewish, Kurdish, Christian, or other minorities in some other Middle Eastern countries were, or still are, as repressive as the Israeli ones. One can also fairly note, without in any way justifying Israeli policies, that since 1977 the Palestinian leadership has squandered opportunities that, if capitalized upon, might have led to a largely satisfactory resolution of the Israeli-Palestinian conflict. What is important for the purpose of this analysis, however, is that these subjective interpretations are part of a widespread system of representations that dominate the symbolic mind of societies and political actors, including the leftist and/or westernized ones. In the absence of a dialogue among nations, these interpretations contribute to the perception of the situation as a totally hopeless one that leaves no chance for peaceful means of action to succeed. Here again, the Palestinian issue plays a decisive role in the formation of this "tragic" worldview so dominant in the Middle East. The fact that the Middle Eastern states, despite having become parts of the world system, with some even having chosen to be close allies of the United States, have been impotent to change the fate of Palestinians, only exacerbates this tendency.

The absurdity of the situation in the Middle East at the beginning of the twenty-first century is illustrated by the fact that one anti-American regime, the Ba'ath regime in Iraq, which had a thoroughly contemptible human rights record, could become the symbol of "Arab resistance," and is glorified both in Palestinian refugee camps and on university campuses all over the Middle East, while the so-called "moderate" states are dismissed as the henchmen of "imperialism" or of the *dar-ul-harb*, the "world of the infidels." If the states choose to view their domestic opponents as "internal enemies," then it is hardly surprising that many political actors, influencing a significant segment of public opinion, in turn look upon the state as nothing more than an internal enemy acting on behalf of external enemies or intruders.

The Regional Violence

Finally, it is important to underscore the fact that for decades violence in the Middle East has not been contained within state borders. Combined with the classical pursuit of arms smuggling, the successive events of the disintegration of the Soviet Union, the Gulf wars, and the Kurdish and Palestinian conflicts have made available abundant amounts of weapons. The inter-state wars and tensions created multiple zones where no internationally recognized state exerts control and where many non-state armed forces have been, and continue to be, active. These zones, often located in the border areas, are propitious for smuggling and commerce of different kinds of instruments of violence.

Moreover, the Middle East, which links Eastern Europe, the former Soviet Union, and Africa, can be considered as a field of economic and symbolic resources. For many decades, the underground economies of the Middle East, not to mention the criminal economies, have been trading in substantial amounts of resources—such as economic resources to conduct covert operations, and weapons, including "weapons of mass destruction"—that cannot be obtained through the legal market economy. These resources possess a natural attraction for non-state actors, whether they are large families, trans-border tribes, political oppositions, or minority actors.

But they are also attractive to the states themselves. In fact, the states, not as institutional organs but as fields of competition divided among different power constituencies, are bound up with this underground economy. The Susurluk and similar scandals in Turkey that I discussed in the second chapter have shown to how great a degree some state-sponsored or protected actors have been involved in drug trafficking. Abundant information also exists on the role of smuggling in the economic health of Saddam Hussein's own family and of the military *muessessa* of Syria. In Algeria, too, smuggling seems to be an important avenue of embourgeoisement.

But the Middle East as a region also holds symbolic resources that have been forbidden or restricted by the states' affiliations. Many sectarian and ethnic groups, in fact, continue to function as trans-border communities. For a Kurdish party in Iraq, Turkey, Iran, or Syria, for instance, it is important to be at once present in the "local" Kurdish sphere determined by the states' borders, and in the regional Kurdish sphere as a whole. The representation and prestige obtained in one of these spheres are used as symbolic capital in the other. Shi'i actors are similarly placed. The Iraqi, Lebanese, Syrian, and Iranian Shi'i spheres are at once autonomous and interdependent. Accordingly, the states themselves cannot act simply within their internationally recognized borders, but must pursue a complex game of patronage relations within the broader region.

Access to these economic and symbolic resources often means playing competitively on an unpredictable field. It requires means, both economic and military, not only to protect one's self, but also to insure resource allocation to others as the price for the patron-client relations they wish to establish. The states play this game much as the non-state actors do. The very logic of the regional game, which recognizes the whole of the Middle East as a field of competition for resources, compels states to undermine and violate the sovereignty of other states. One can cite many examples to illustrate this transgression of international law by the states themselves. To name just a few, during the last two decades Turkey, Iran, Iraq, and Syria have all, at one moment or another, militarily supported the Kurdish subjects of other states. Turkey continues to support, at least economically, the Turkoman community of Iraq. Iran, over the past two decades, has militarily supported the Shi'i groups in the region; and other examples abound.

From Structured Violence to Privatized Violence

Highly unstable domestic politics, a political culture that legitimizes violence as the founding act of politics, and violent regional competition all together constitute the structural factors behind the phenomenon of mass violence in at least six Middle Eastern countries (Syria, Iraq, Iran, Turkey, Egypt, and Algeria).

Each situation must, of course, be analyzed in itself, and due attention must be given to the particular domestic conditions and historical configurations which led to the emergence of violence. It is, however, important to note that the waves of violence that struck the above listed countries, even those waves that started spontaneously, all shared at least one technical commonality: they were quickly under the control of and conducted by more or less institutionalized structures. Organizations employed violence instrumentally in the hopes of achieving a goal.

Except in Iran, where the unrest led to the Islamic revolution, these movements shared also a second common point: they failed to provoke major political changes in their societies. They did not weaken the states' coercive capabilities, nor did they lead to revolutions. On the contrary, many Middle Eastern states proved quite capable of combining the tools of coercion and patron-client relations to boost their resilience. After the years of instability in the 1950s and 1960s, many regimes of the Middle East emerged largely or completely intact. The violence did not stimulate collective reflection within society upon the structural reasons behind it, or upon the political blockages and crises that the states used as a new social engineering technique. Civil society throughout the Middle East remained quite weak, and was unable to produce political alternatives to state coercion and political violence.

Many reasons account for the resilience of the state, the failure of the violent opposition movements, and the all but non-existent role of civil society. As I have already observed, although the societies rejected the official unanimisms of the states, they did not accept the counter-unanimisms that the actors of violence proposed to them. The violent oppositions failed to win the trust or support of their societies at large because the societies regarded them as just as "foreign" as the state officialdom. They were incapable of resolving the most urgent problems of what they conceived to be the populace, and the populace refused to allow those movements to represent them before the state. In Egypt, for example, the residents of the suburbs preferred their local dignitaries to Islamist revolutionaries as interlocutors with the state. The states, on the other hand, efficiently combined coercion and resource allocation. The combination of these two techniques intimidated many segments of the societies and allowed others to ally with the state and collect a sort of security rent.

And, as noted earlier, the states increased their own resources. Rents from petroleum, for example, greatly bolstered the Iraqi and Algerian regimes. The security rents strengthened the Turkish, Syrian, and Egyptian regimes. Thus, the states gained significant financial autonomy and could become quite insensitive to the social effects of violence.

So-called "markets of violence"[115] also played a role—or one should say a double role—in the reproduction and the regulation of violence. First, they allowed the states to control access to important sums of undeclared resources; as the Turkish, Iraqi, and Syrian cases attest, these resources were used to create and bolster patron-client relations and to finance illicit coercive policies. Second, they also granted loyal non-state actors freer access to economic resources. For many actors involved in the "markets of violence," insuring their own durability became more important than the realization of their political goals. "Markets of violence" thus permitted the institutionalization of violence, but at the cost of its de-politicization.

Finally, the Middle Eastern societies have accepted a limited level of institutionalized violence and coercion and have grown accustomed to living with them. In all the cases mentioned above, the youth constituted the pivotal force in the violent struggles. But the violence found very little effective support among other, broader social strata. The economical *infitah* (transition to privatized economy) has in fact provided these societies with access, at different levels, to the benefits of the informal economy, and thereby has made less urgent any need for elaborating political alternatives to state coercion and to violence.

Only in-depth case studies and comparative research on the many violent conflicts in the Middle East will corroborate, or disprove, the hypotheses suggested above. But if they are corroborated, they may explain why violence in the Middle East has been changing its form during the last few years. The perpetrators of violence are becoming more and more interested in ensuring their own durability and in integrating into the underground economy than they are in changing regimes. They remain efficient organized forces, and they continue to legitimize their violence with political and ideological discourses. And there is still an unmistakable link between their discourses and their praxes. But at the same time, the violence they perpetrate is becoming more and more privatized and less and less politically committed. Privatizing violence for them means making it more professional, more rational, and more cost-effective. As with economic activities or patron-client-patron networks, violence has to pay off and must yield a tangible benefit. The Algerian case, where the perpetrators of violence include different GIA groups, militia forces, and the more or less independent security detachments, shows that this privatized form of violence can aim primarily at winning goods and land rather than creating political change. My impression is that it is the institutionalization (i.e., professionalization and privatization) of violence, rather than a misreading of the structural factors behind the violence, that explains the apparent pacification of the Middle East and decrease of mass violence there.

Radicalization and Self-Sacrifice

It is important to understand that this general process of the institutionalization and professionalization of violence in the Middle East has gone hand-in-hand with an extreme radicalization of some fragments. One can observe this radicalization in different areas of the Middle East. The supra-territorial al-Qaida is now surely the best-known example. But Gama'a in Egypt, Dev-Sol in Turkey, the Hizbullah or Jund-al-Islam in Turkish and Iraqi Kurdistan, as well as some Palestinian groups, are other examples of this acme of radicalization.

Of course, we must not blithely assume these organizations are related. On the contrary, it is important to analyze the history of each to understand their respective evolutions and particular objectives. It is also obvious that the constraints under which they operate are very different, and that they do not possess comparable prospects for peaceful integration.[116] However, they do share at least one critical commonality: the readiness of their members to commit self-sacrificial acts of violence.

One may object that, in the cases of al-Qaida, the Palestinian groups (both Islamist and non-Islamist), and Dev-Sol, radicalization has not been accompanied by a de-institutionalized violence. Certainly it is true that in the two first cases, the most extreme forms of violence, those involving self-destruction, are organized and carried out by bureaucratic structures, and in the case of Dev-Sol a bureaucratic structure encourages such suicidal violence. But it is the individual readiness of their militants to destroy themselves in order to give a meaning to their *da'wa*, and not the bureaucratic organization and screening of their deaths, which gives a meaning to this radicalization. Violence itself is reproduced because of the availability of these militants to use their bodies as both a weapon and a message. No one, not even the most cynical bureaucratic apparatus, can buy or sell this weapon, and no one can use it without the consent of the weapon itself.

Therefore, the main enigma is not the structures of the bureaucratic organizations that take charge of this violence, but rather the extreme individualization of the violence itself. How do people become mentally prepared to destroy themselves? How does the militant's willingness to destroy him or herself survive the conditions of prolonged mixed socialization, as was the case with the al-Qaida hijackers? How one can prepare his or her own self-destruction—in other words, the destruction of his or her individual time, within the framework of a universal time—for a sustained period of 5–6 months without one's resolve weakening?

We must admit that those questions, fundamental for future research on violence, cannot yet be answered.[117] But one thing does seem obvious: one cannot easily assimilate this individualized violence into a rationally founded or instrumental violence. As I maintained earlier, a rational or instrumental violence aims ultimately at political change or at the construction of new power relations. Even in the case of failure, it can metamorphose into a privatized violence that still retains a rational, instrumental basis. Self-destruction, however, eliminates the entire equation of power, leaving no room for goals other than the act of self-destruction itself.

Individualized violence that leads to the destruction of oneself seems to be a reaction to the limits of collective violence. As I discussed above, attacking the symbols and presence of the dominant political systems did not lead the "masses" of the Middle East to join in violent opposition struggles. And the states ultimately proved to be much more effective in marshaling and wielding coercion than expected. The passage from the *foci*[118] kind of violence to revolution did not go any farther in the Middle East than it did in Latin America. Even in those places where violence was linked to a national question, and where the majority of a given population massively supported it, as in the cases of the Palestinians and the Kurds, the violent opposition movements lacked the material conditions to change power relations. Elsewhere, the material conditions for the reproduction of violence decreased drastically.

In many cases in the Middle East, in fact, violent movements have lasted over one or two decades. This is a very long period in an individual's life. Militants who were 20 years old when they first joined a struggle are already between the ages of 30 and 40 when the cycle of collective violence ends. That is often considered to be the age of maturity that follows that of youthful enthusiasm. Most of these militants have the options of either becoming "mature" and acknowledging the futility of their own violent action, or of being co-opted without attaining any of their goals. Moreover, the relative flexibility of the political or religious fields in Turkey, Algeria, Egypt, and the Gulf countries allows many leftist or Islamist militants to become official and tolerated figures of a diluted, henceforth solely symbolic opposition. Upon reaching the age of maturity, other militants grow cynical, yet comprehend the utility of violence as an instrument and as a technique for accessing resources. Thus, these militants opt for a privatized form of violence.

For reasons that have not yet been studied, some militants develop a tragic vision of the world in which violence, even at its most unfruitful, remains the only answer to the world. Many militants fail to remake themselves either by being co-opted into the existing political system, or by becoming perpetrators of a privatized form of violence. Some of these, at least, are targeted as useful internal enemies, and so have very weak prospects for integration into the established political system. More often, though, they have internalized the sacralized messages and symbols of the "cause," and are imbued with a deep fidelity to the martyrs' memory. There was — and still is — an obvious tension between the rational choices of many militants, who ultimately accept integration without attaining any of their goals, and the fidelity of many others toward the messages, symbols, and duties of their sacralized *da'wa*.

Moreover, while this process of the maturation of the older generations takes place, new members continue to join the struggle. These newcomers are born into the violence or were very young at its beginning. For them, the discourse, symbols, and auras of holiness that surrounded their childhood and adolescence are not empty words that one can exchange in the "markets of violence." Rather, they are sacrosanct blocks.[119] The construction of oneself takes place in the framework of these blocks alone. In such a situation one cannot project oneself as an individual, but only as a part of a collectivity, itself heightened to an absolute, to some extent immaterial, principle. This principle may be religious, national, or secular. The absolute faith in this principle, however, can only lead to disillusionment, particularly in the case of a campaign of mass violence that fails. The consequences of this disillusion are aggravated by the absence of any positive individual or collective horizons.

In the wake of collective violence's failure or its privatization, and the subsequent disillusion, violence can retain a meaning and be reproduced only if it takes a self-sacrificial form, or if it wins a messianic, eschatological dimension. Self-sacrificial forms of violence aim at testifying to the innocence of the *subject* and his or her preserved purity rather than attaining any earthly goal. One's own destruction attests to his or her refusal to accept any compromise with the order, not only the existing political and social order, but with *any* political and social order. In some cases, this refusal can be explained by the attractiveness of a religious appeal and the divinely promised compensation in eternal peace. But for some left-wing militants at least, the sacredness of a cause or a principle itself replaces the religious appeal. The militant's self-destruction becomes the only way to resolve the tension between the quest for purity and the corruption of the world, including the corruption of former comrades. Even where the self-destruction is supervised by an organization, it seems to be linked to this kind of quest for the absolute. Sociologically speaking, the actors involved in such a quest become subjects under the condition of their own destruction.

But an instrumental violence that has failed to achieve its goals and is condemned to decline as a collective movement can also produce an apocalyptic form of violence. As is well known, messianism is intimately linked to the perception that the world order is drawing to its end, and that the establishment of a new order of heavenly peace on earth, i.e., a non-earthly order on the earth itself, is imminent. But this peace can be established only at the price of a preliminary eschatological violence. The earth becomes the field of the realization of projects decided by heaven. The human beings of the earth are thus called to become the soldiers of God. They cease to be actors, and they are not required to become sociological subjects. A soldier of God is an *actent*, i.e. a henchman in a manifestation of violence directed from heaven. Mortal men and women perpetrate the violence, but it is not

134

a human violence; it is a divine one and it accepts no judgment by earthly authorities. It is obvious that in this repertoire of violence, self-sacrifice constitutes an important dimension. The *actents* trust either in the invincibility granted to them by God, or in a heavenly imminent recompense. Hence death is either non-existent or irrelevant.

Understanding how these kinds of violence lead to self-sacrifice requires, naturally, a comparative prosopography. We lack for now the instruments necessary for such a study. The elements currently at our disposal suggest, however, that the usual sociological categories are of very limited use for comprehending self-sacrificial violence. The social origins of the militants involved in such violence, for instance, are not *systematically* relevant. For instance, many of the members of the PKK and Dev-Sol who opted for the self-sacrificial forms of violence are of poor social origins, but not all. In the Palestinian case, the authors of the suicidal attacks do not belong to the poorest milieus. Female militants are heavily present among them; in the case of the PKK, women initiated the suicide attacks. Some of these PKK militants came from the countryside, but others did not. Although the majority of Palestinian suicide bombers are young men, among their ranks have also been found a 27-year-old female nurse and a 45-year-old landowner.

The most significant case that illustrates the fragility of the explanations linking violence to socioeconomic conditions or the usual sociological categories is of course that of the hijackers of September 11. Their case demonstrates that during the 1980s and 1990s, together with a radicalism of the poor, a second radicalism, this one of the rich, emerged in the Middle East. This radicalism took on a deeply apocalyptic shape and therefore became infinitely more impressive than the violence of the previous radical Islamist organizations. Almost all the members of al-Qaida who participated to the September 11 attacks were from sociologically "healthy" milieus, or at least they enjoyed a high standard of living in comparison to the other members of their generations. Many of them were active in the field of science or had a scientific background. Unlike the PKK or Dev-Sol members, who were socialized in an autarkic environment, or the Palestinian suicide bombers who grew up under occupation, they were all socialized, for long periods, in mixed environments.

This may be not be surprising. In fact, one can maintain that there is no cognitive incompatibility between scientific training and an absolute trust in a non-earthly mission. Similarly, theirs is only one case of many of radicalism of rich people in world history. The studies of Norman Cohn suggest that, although not a sociological category, the "rich" constituted the category of the "announcers" in many messianic movements in the European history.[120] The invention of meanings, including apocalyptic ones, does not require only a firm belief, a dogma. It also requires instruments for the intellectual re-appropriation, re-interpretation, and codification of meanings. These kinds of intellectual processes have always required people capable of commenting upon and contesting present meanings, and of inventing new meanings.

It is obviously too early to say whether these forms of individualized, self-sacrificial violence or apocalyptic forms of violence will or will not become banal patterns of violence in the coming years. One should, however, bear in the mind that a rational/instrumental violence with a political, social, economic finality might, as a result of its incapacity to attend its aims, always switch to a nihilistic or messianic self-sacrificial form of violence.

But nihilism and messianism themselves might become impossible to reproduce in time. The actors using nihilistic or messianic forms of violence are obliged either to suppress themselves or to give a meaning to their action, and ultimately, to reinvent hope. One can imagine that this process of inventing hope will also lead in the Middle East to the invention of nonviolent forms of action.

Conclusion

I have suggested that there is a link between violence on the one hand and the incapacity of the Middle Eastern states to legitimize conflicts, create democratic spaces, and integrate political, social, and communal actors on the other. While influenced and shaped by power relations, violence in the Middle East is also rooted in the regime opponents' perceptions of the forms of domination and syntaxes of hegemony as "unacceptable" or even as "incredible." In the Arab Middle East, perceptions of recent history, and especially of the Palestinian issue, have also facilitated the radicalization of violent opposition movements. The regimes close to the United States of America are regarded with contempt and dismissed as the servile lackeys of the powers dividing and dominating the Muslim world.

For decades, the option of violence was a rational or instrumental one. The perpetrators of violence either aimed to access social, political, and cultural resources, or to change the structure of the power relations. In any case, they offered alternative meanings and narratives (nationalism, socialism, Islamism, etc.) that were accepted as "credible" by some sections of their societies.

But no campaign of violence can last forever. As a consequence of the states' proven vigor in the face of opposition movements, the generalized social fatigue that we observe in many countries in the

139

Middle East, and generational change, violent mass movements were declining at the turn of the new century. But this did not mean the end of violence. Instead, new forms of violence emerged. In some places, privatized and professionalized forms of violence replaced the previous collective ones. In other cases, individualized or collective, but much more radical, zealous, non-earthly, and eschatological forms of violence emerged. The perpetrators of these forms of violence sacralized their founding utopia, as well as the duty of fidelity towards principles and martyrs. They eventually embraced the notion of destroying their own bodies as the only remaining way to testify to their own integrity and innocent, uncorrupted character. Even more than the previous forms of violence, which took even more human lives, this kind of violence contributed and contributes to the banalization of death.

It is too early to predict whether these forms of violence constitute only the last, flickering flames of the preceding campaigns of mass violence, which are waning, or whether they herald a new era that will be marked by new waves of mass violence. Many things will naturally depend on the political and military evolution in the region as well as on the reactions of the Middle Eastern societies and of the different strata that compose them. One can reasonably predict that, given the complex webs of power relations, the subjective perceptions of the actors, and symbolic values like fidelity to martyrs and desire for revenge, violence will not entirely disappear, at least for the foreseeable future, from the political arenas of the Middle East.

But violence is not fated or inevitable. The political imagination can produce both region-wide alternatives and political solutions for each country individually. Only the existence of alternatives to violence will unmask violence, demystify it, and render it less attractive. These alternatives should render dignity to the marginalized groups and communities, and, broadly speaking, to the Middle East as a whole. They should not shy away from legitimizing conflicts and divisions as parts of any society. Rather than suppress these tensions, they should open the path to the political integration of the actors who are the protagonists of these conflicts. But such processes require, naturally, both internationally legitimized instances of arbitration and radical changes and reforms in the domestic political arenas of the Middle Eastern societies.

Appendix

A Brief Comment on Methodology

Necessary conditions for the emergence of collective violence:

- Absence of a contractual framework

- Refusal to recognize social, political, sectarian, communitarian divisions

- Refusal to legitimize conflicts

The methodology used in this book is a provisional one. I developed it during the spring semester of 2002 as part of my teaching at the Ecole des Hautes Etudes en Sciences Sociales.

The main analytical concern of this "multi-variant"[121] model is to explain the nihilistic/self-sacrificial and apocalyptic forms of violence. The model includes, however, also a third repertoire, which is more familiar to scholars: the rational and/or instrumental forms of violence. This repertoire can be considered as the known term of the equation, which helps to define the two other unidentified terms.

I applied seven criteria to compare these repertoires. (See table, pp. 144–45.) The first criterion concerns the goals of the violence. In the first repertoire, the perpetrators of violence aim to replace the exist-

Table of Criteria and Forms/Repertoires of Violence

CRITERIA FORMS / REPERTOIRES OF VIOLENCE	*Goals*	*Status of the authors of violence*	*Regimes of despair and hope; regimes of meaning*
Rational / instrumental violence	Construction of a new world order	Collective actors capable of organizing new power relations	Despair concerning the existing world order; hope in a coming world order
Nihilistic / self-sacrificial violence	Denunciation of the world order	Negative subject Self-destruction as the only condition of emerging as subject	Despair concerning the current world order and the impossibility of replacing it with another world order; no hope
Messianic violence	Construction of a heavenly order on earth	*Actents* and not actors or subjects	Despair concerning the world order; total hope in a coming eschatological order

Temporality	Status of risk in the action	Scale of maximal violence	Universal aspects (reproducible in more than one culture or time-space)
Tabula rasa as the condition of restoring history	Risk is not denied. Individuals enter into action not to die, but with the prospect for survival and victory.	Massive, but gradual and fragmented. Perpetrators of violence have to multiply the repertoires of their action, as well as the fronts. Necessity of detachments of fighters.	Transformation of violence into state coercive power. Reconstruction of politics on the base of enmity.
Absence of landmarks giving sense to the past. Impossibility of reconstructing history. Destruction of time.	In the case of violence targetting only someone else: no projection of victory. In the case of self-sacrifice: suppression of the risk for oneself.	Individual or weakly collective. Violence is often reduced to a single action or to a series of non-articulated actions.	Individual. Desire to redeem oneself from the inherent corruption of the world and testify to one's individual innocence through self-sacrifice.
Suppression of world temporality and its replacement by a heavenly non-time	Denial of personal risk; transformation of God and the "chosen" in recompense or protector	Total violence. No possible comparison with human-scale violence (eschatological violence). Absolute terror when conditions allow it.	Idea of invincibility of the "chosen" and/or the fighters. Heavenly recompense following death.

ing political, social, and/or economic order with a new one. Those of the second repertoire denounce the existing earthly order, but have no hope or belief in the possibility of being able to replace it with any other alternative order. Their self-destruction is the only response they can give to the world order. Those of the last repertoire reject any earthly order constructed by mortals, and prepare for the arrival of a heavenly order on earth.

The second criterion defines the sociological status of the perpetrators of violence. In the case of the first repertoire, we have collective actors. The logic of this repertoire demands the existence of political parties, guerrilla organizations, or clandestine groups capable of organizing complex power relations through the use of violence and of operating in multiple fields. In the second repertoire, individual subjects often replace collective actors. These subjects are negative ones in the sense that they cannot place their actions in a positive construction. The status of subject is obtained almost on the condition of his/her own suppression. In the millenarian repertoire, we find *actents*, and not actors, in the sense that they believe themselves to be soldiers of a divine project.

The third criterion concerns the regime of hope or hopelessness. In the first repertoire, the actors have no more hope in the capacity of the present world order to satisfy their expectations. But they are confident in another earthly order that they aim to construct. In the second repertoire, the subjects are desperate about the existing political, social, and economic order, but they do not believe in or look to a coming or even possible world order. In the last repertoire, the perpetrators hold no hope in any earthly order, but possess a vibrant hope in the coming of an eschatological order.

The fourth criterion concerns temporality. In the first repertoire, the accessible past is commonly regarded as a period of corruption, while the forgotten "golden age" (primitive communism, the original community, *asr-i Sa'ada* ...) is taken as the true History. This History has been interrupted by the past, which was marked by the abandonment of the original purity of the Golden Age. The *tabula rasa* will thus make possible the obliteration of the past so that History can start again and fulfill its meaning. In the second repertoire, the individual subject is unable to move between his or her different temporalities, the universal temporality, group temporality (or temporalities), and his or her own individual temporality. He or she is unable to mentally organize the past according to more or less significant landmarks, and cannot give a sense to the future by projecting him or herself in a constructive way. The destruction of time becomes the only remaining solution. In the last repertoire, the world temporality, i.e. time itself, is destroyed and replaced by a heavenly non-temporal order.

The fifth criterion concerns, once again, a key concept of sociology, which is the notion of risk. In the case of the rational/instrumental repertoire of violence, risk plays a decisive role. The employment of violence itself involves accepting risks, including the risk of death, but it does not preclude consideration of the prospects for survival and participation in coming victories with one's fellow-fighters. In the second repertoire, particularly when the violence becomes self-sacrificial, the notion of risk is entirely absent, the authors of violence having no prospects of survival or sharing in the fruits of a coming victory. In the last case, risk loses meaning. The "Chosen" can face no risk. Protected by God, they may become shields who protects their militants.

The sixth criterion concerns the potential scale of violence. Rational/instrumental violence may be massive. But even when it is very deadly, it is gradual and fragmented. The collective actors are obliged to operate on a multitude of fields and fronts. In the second repertoire, the perpetrator may be a single individual, but the victims can be many. Particularly when it takes on a sacrificial character, violence can be limited to but a single action. This action, which entails self-destruction, allows the negative subject to testify to his or her absolute faith in a cause or to buy his or her innocence in a completely corrupted world. Finally, in the case of the apocalyptic repertoire, violence is eschatological. Its maximum potential scale can by no means be compared to the violence exerted by the human beings. The attacks of September 11 had precisely this "incomparable" dimension.

The last criterion concerns the universals of the violence. All three repertoires are universal and possess common characteristics that are found well beyond the bounds of Muslim (or any other single) culture. The rational/instrumental repertoire aims at the transformation of struggle into power or into "force" as it is defined in Sorelian terminology. It aims to re-construct politics, albeit on a basis which includes a new equation of enmity. In the second repertoire, the subjects aim to redeem themselves from the inherently corrupted world and testify to their innocence through violence and self-sacrifice. This last repertoire cultivates the idea of "the Chosen" and apocalyptic terror.

I would like to note that this typology of violence is an ideal-type typology, in the sense that Max Weber gave to this concept. In reality, of course, the organizations and groups employing violence are complex, and are even at times capable of mobilizing, at different levels and places, the three repertoires at the same time. In the case of al-

Qaida, for example, the available information suggests that the organization had a three-level structure. Osama bin Laden, who was at the top level, seems to be the leading figure, having at once a very cynical and mystical, not to say millenarian, world vision. At the intermediary level, the organization possessed a highly rationalized bureaucracy capable both of organizing sophisticated attacks and realizing very lucrative economic transactions up until the attacks against the Twin Towers. At the lower level figured the rank-and-file militants, among them some very well-educated individuals, who were ready to die for the sacredness of the cause or for the messianic appeal.

Likewise, perpetrators of violence might switch from one repertoire to another. It happens quite often that instrumental/rational violence fails to achieve its goals. The perpetrators are thus obliged to switch either to an institutionalized violence as in Colombia, or to a privatized violence, as in many Middle Eastern countries. Or they can commit themselves to different forms of nihilistic/sacrificial forms of violence. As I suggested previously, the nihilistic/sacrificial forms violence are committed by single individuals. Their reproduction in time, however, can give birth to either messianism or rational/instrumental violence. Finally, the apocalyptic forms of violence can produce either an institutionalized/rationalized violence or a new religiosity, capable of producing internal coercive mechanisms.

Notes

1. L'École des hautes études en sciences sociales, Paris.
2. Institut d'études sur l'Islam et les sociétés du monde musulman, Paris.
3. English and French do not have a polysemous term comparable to *Gewalt* in German, which means violence, force, constraint, and coercion. I have followed Charles Tilly's example and used the term "coercion" to define the set of constraints and physical violence employed by the state, while applying the term "violence" to the physically destructive acts of non-state actors and individuals.
4. Hannah Arendt, "A Special Supplement: Reflections on Violence," *The New York Review of Books* 12, no. 4 (February 27, 1969), later published as "On Violence," in *Crises of the Republic* (New York: Harcourt Brace Jovanovich, 1972).
5. Encylopaedia Universalis, *Dictionnaire de la sociologie* (Paris: Albin Michel, 1998).
6. R. Boudon et al., *Dictionnaire de Sociologie* (Paris: Larousse, 1999).
7. Charles Tilly, *Coercion, Capital, and European States, AD 990–1990* (Oxford: Basil Blackwell, 1991); "War Making and State Making as Organised Crime," in P. Evans, D. Rueschemeyer and T. Skocpol, eds., *Bringing the State Back In* (Cambridge: Cambridge University Press, 1985), pp. 169–91.
8. Ted Robert Gurr, *Why Do Men Rebel?* (Princeton: Princeton University Press, 1970).
9. M. Wieviorka, *La violence en France* (Paris: Seuil, 1999).
10. Georg Simmel, *Conflict: The Web of Group Affiliations* (New York: Free Press, 1955).
11. The expression is suggested by Michael Billig, *Banal Nationalism* (London: Sage Publications, 1995).

12. On the use of culture in the explanation of violence in the Basque Country in Spain, see M. Wieviorka, *E.T.A. et la violence politique au Pays-Basque espagnol* (Geneva: UNRISD, 1993).

13. P. Haenni, *Banlieues indociles? Sur la politisation des quartiers peri-urbains du Caire* (unpublished Ph.D. thesis, Paris, IEP, 2001).

14. On the privatization of violence, see M. Wieviorka, ed., *Pour un nouveau paradigme de la violence* (Paris: L'Harmattan, 1998).

15. F. Jean and J.-C. Ruffin, eds., *Économies des guerres civiles* (Paris: Hachette-Pluriel, 1996); J. Hannoyer, ed., *Guerres civiles. Economies de la violence, dimensions de la civilité* (Paris: Karthala-Cermoc, 1999); G. Elwert, S. Feuchwang, and D. Neubert, eds., *Dynamics of Violence. Process of Escalation and De-escalation in Violent Conflicts* (Berlin: Duncker and Humboldt, 1999).

16. Shortly after the September 11 attacks, the French philosopher J. Baudriard (*L'esprit du terrorisme*, Paris: Galilée, 2002) drew attention to their nihilistic aspects. André Glucksmann proposed a similar (although a less original) reading: *Dostoïevski à Manhattan* (Paris: Robert Laffont, 2002).

17. A. Camus, *L'homme révolté* (Paris: NRF, 1985 [first published in 1951]).

18. F. Khosrokhavar's analysis of the "martyrs" of the Iran-Iraq War: *L'utopie sacrifiée. Sociologie de la révolution iranienne* (Paris: FNSP, 1993).

19. O. Roy, *L'échec de l'islam politique* (Paris: Seuil, 1992); G. Kepel, *Jihad* (Paris: NRF/Folio, 2001).

20. K. Makiya & H. Mneimneh, "Manual for a Raid," *The New York Review of Books* 49, no. 1 (2002): 18–20. For instance, in his testimony, one of the hijackers emphasized that his body should be washed with *eau de cologne*. As is well known, martyrs in the Muslim tradition are buried with their clothes. They are considered to have testified to the unity of God and the prophecy of Muhammad with their own death. Being already in Paradise, they are not required to face the Final Judgment.

21. Anfal, meaning "booty" (title of a verse in the Qur'an), was the code-name of a series of operations planned by Saddam Hussein's regime in 1988. They aimed at the destruction of the Kurdish countryside. See Human Rights Watch, *Iraq's Crime of Genocide: The Anfal Campaign Against the Kurds* (London: Yale University Press, 1995).

22. J.C. Randal, *After Such Knowledge What Forgiveness? My Encounters with Kurdistan* (New York: Farrar, Strauss and Giroux, 1997).

23. S. Çelik, *Ağrı Dağını Taşımak. Çağdaş Kürt Halk Direnişi, Siyasi, Askeri, Ekonomik ve Toplumsal Sonuçları* (Frankfurt: Zambon, 2000), pp. 506–509.

24. Many people committed suicide after Öcalan decided to stop the armed struggle. Suicide then became a mass phenomenon, particularly among the women in the Batman province where the PKK was the dominant actor. The available documentation, however, does not allow us to directly link these suicides to Öcalan's decision. See M. Halis, *Batman'da Kadınlar Ölüyor* (Istanbul: Metis, 2001).

25. For this concept, see Şerif Mardin, *Türk Modernleşmesi: Makaleler 4* (Istanbul: İletişim, 1991, p. 108).

26. Stephen Helmsley Longrigg, *Iraq, 1900 to 1950: A Political, Social and Economic History* (Oxford: Oxford University Press, 1953).

27. Quoted by C. Celil, *XIX. Yüzyil Osmanlı Imparatorluğu'nda Kürtler* (Ankara: Öz-Ge, 1992).

28. David Kushner, *The Rise of Turkish Nationalism, 1876–1908* (London: Frank Cass, 1977).

29. For documents, see M. Bayrak, *Kürtler ve Ulusal Demokratik Mücadeleleri. Gizli Belgeler – Araştırmalar - Notlar* (Ankara: Öz-Ge, 1993); M. Bayrak, *Açık-Gizli/Resmi-Gayriresmi Kürdoloji Belgeleri* (Ankara: Öz-Ge, 1994).

30. E. Copeaux, *Une vision turque du monde à travers les cartes de 1931 à nos jours* (Paris: CNRS Éditions, 2000). Later on, in Syria, during the constitution of the so-called Arab-Belt in 1963 across the borders with Turkey, the Kurds have been presented as a negative atavistic group. See Ch. Vanly, *Le problème kurde en Syrie* (Comité Pour la Défense du Peuple kurde, 1968).

31. For the conditions of the emergence of this intelligentsia and its features, see S. Othman, "Mulakhaza tarikhiyya nachat al-harakat al-kawmiyya al-kurdiya" (Historical Observations on the Genesis of the Kurdish Nationalist Movement), *Studia Kurdica,* no. 1 (1984): 20–32. (I thank Dr. Othman for providing me with an English version of this article.)

32. For more on the Anfal operations, see J. Goldberg, "The Great Terror," *The New Yorker,* March 25, 2002, 52–75.

33. In 1994, for instance, the General Staff of the Turkish armed forces accused H. Mezarcı and some ten other deputies of Turkish Assembly of being "perverse." The deputies had supported the rehabilitation of opponents of the Kemalist regime who were executed in 1926. Many newspapers also denounced the "perversity" of the deputies. See H.

Bozarslan, "Parler de la corde dans la maison du pendu," *CEMOTI,* no. 18 (1994): 339–51.

34. Şerif Mardin, "The Nakşibendi Order in Turkish History," in R. Tapper, *Islam in Modern Turkey. Religion, Politics and Literature in a Secular State* (London: I.B. Tauris, 1991), p. 122.
35. Tens of members of the legal pro-Kurdish parties as well as a deputy of the DEP (Democratic Party) were killed during the 1990s.
36. For more, see H.J. Barkey and G.E. Fuller, *Turkey's Kurdish Question* (New York: Rowman and Littlefield Publishers Inc., 1998).
37. Ch. Tilly, "War Making and State Making as Organised Crime."
38. Among others, see P. Bourdieu and J. D. Wacquant, *Réponses. Pour une anthropologie réflexive* (Paris: Seuil, 1992).
39. This concept is suggested by Erik H. Erikson in his *Identity, Youth and Crisis* (New York: W.W. Norton and Company, 1968).
40. "Happy is he/she who says 'I am a Turk!'" is one of the most oft-quoted adages of M. K. Atatürk.
41. For more on the PKK of the 1980s and 1990s, see Paul J. White, *Primitive Rebels or Revolutionary Modernizers? The Kurdish National Movement in Turkey* (London: Zed Press, 2000); Martin van Bruinessen, "Between Guerrilla War and Political Murder: The Workers' Party of Kurdistan," *MERIP Report* (July–August 1988): 40–46; C. Kutschera, "Révélations sur le système Öcalan," *Confluences Méditerranée,* no. 34 (2000): 113–17.
42. See my *La question kurde: Etats et minorités au Moyen-Orient* (Paris, Presses de Sciences-Po, 1997).
43. In 1958, Franz Fanon, one of the theoreticians of the Algerian War of Independence, promoted violence in order to build a de-colonized *country* (F. Fanon, *Sociologie d'une révolution,* Paris: Petite Collection Maspero, 1982). Two years later, however, Fanon was promoting total violence as the only condition for the invention of de-colonized *men.* In fact, Fanon was frightened by the prospect of a victory that would lead to the state's independence without changing the society or men, as had been the case in some de-colonized African countries. This fear seems to explain, at least partly, his move from an instrumental violence to a total violence (F. Fanon, *Les damnés de la Terre,* Paris: Petite Collection Maspero, 1974).
44. For the role of Öcalan's charisma in the Kurdish movement, see P. White, *Primitive Rebels or Revolutionary Modernizers?*

45. In 1993, Öcalan did stop fighting for a couple of months. Before any concrete steps could be taken, however, President Özal, who had wanted to introduce some reforms, died. Demirel, the new President, was less enthusiastic about negotiations. That same year, Şemdin Sakık, one of Öcalan's commanders, unilaterally started the war, thereby putting Öcalan himself in a very difficult position before the Turkish authorities.

46. As Öcalan and the party press acknowledged, many executions took place within the organization. As a result of changes in the party's internal power-relations, some executed militants have been rehabilitated, and their executors in turn have been executed. See the party's official organ, *Serxwebun* (September 1992 and August 1993), for the biographies of some of the "rehabilitated" members proclaimed "martyrs."

47. Many of these nationalists had been active during the 1960s and 1970s. At the beginning of the guerrilla war, they were very reluctant to join the PKK. But with the intensification of the war, many of them joined the organization, either for emotional reasons or to boost their own prestige.

48. This was the case for Sakık.

49. G. D. Brockett, "Collective Action and the Turkish Revolution: Towards a Framework for the Social History of the Atatürk era, 1923–1938," in Sylvia Kedouri, ed., *Turkey Before and After Atatürk. Internal and External Affairs* (London: Frank Cass, 1999), pp. 44–66.

50. For published documents on this topic see Aydınlık Yayınları, *Resmi Belgelerle Kontrgerilla ve MHP. I. Kitap: CIA'nin Türkiye'deki Kontrgerilla Teorisi ve Uygulaması* (Istanbul: Aydınlık Yayınları, 1978), especially p. 45.

51. G. Zileli, *Havariler* (Istanbul: İletişim, 2002).

52. These Arrows are nationalism, republicanism, revolutionism, populism, secularism, and etatism.

53. Şerif Mardin, "Youth and Violence in Turkey," *International Social Science Journal* 1, no. 2 (1977): 229–54.

54. Ibid.

55. Ziya Gökalp (1876–1924) was one of the main Turkish nationalist thinkers of the Unionist period (1908–1918).

56. Mayors enjoyed great autonomy in the use of their municipalities' resources, and could freely appoint their clients to key positions in the

city administration and distribute jobs to their supporters. They also
had indirect control over the recruitment policy of the state enterprises
in their territorial jurisdiction. Finally, more than the state-appointed
governors, mayors were in charge of the organization of everyday life,
as well as official ceremonies and celebrations of holidays such as
National Liberation Day. The mayors possessed the authority to select
the uniforms to be worn as well as the slogans, music, and images
that gave the celebrations their political character. See H. Bozarslan,
"Le phénomène milicien: une composante de la violence politique en
Turquie des années 70," *Turcica* 31 (1999): 185–244.

57. *Hemşehrilik*: the link of solidarity between people who have the same
geographic background.

58. T.C. Ankara-Çankiri-Kastamonu İlleri Sıkıyönetim Komutanlığı
Askeri Savcılığı, *İddianame THKP/C Devrimci-Yol* 1 (1982). One
should naturally be very careful concerning the information given by
military prosecutors, who declared the indicted persons to be "internal
enemies."

59. Many observers thought that the 1977 elections would allow a
governmental change and bring the Republican People's Party of B.
Ecevit in power. But Ecevit's party could not obtain a parliamentary
majority. A second "Nationalist Front" coalition led by Süleyman
Demirel, and in which the Nationalist Action Party (MHP) of Colonel
Türkeş participated, was formed. The MHP presented itself as the main
challenger to the left and stepped up its violent operations. Pogroms and
killings of well-known liberal politicians, academics, and journalists
increased.

60. For the figures, see H. Bozarslan, "Le phénomène milicien."

61. For Abdullah Çatli's biography see H. Bozarslan, *Network-Building,
Ethnicity and Violence in Turkey* (Abu Dhabi: ECSSR, 1999).

62. For this notion, meaning social acceptance of deviant forms of action,
see E. Erikson, *Identity, Youth and Crisis*.

63. D. Pecault, "Violence et politique: quatre éléments de réflexion à propos
de la Colombie," *Cultures et Conflits,* nos. 13–14 (1994): 157.

64. J.B. Rule, *Theories of Civil Violence* (Berkeley, Calif.: University of
California Press, 1988).

65. H. Bozarslan, "La crise comme instrument politique en Turquie,"
Esprit, no. 1 (2001): 145–57.

66. Many journalists who write for *Cumhuriyet, Aydınlık,* and *Hürriyet,* all
newspapers close to the state, use the term *liboş*, a highly pejorative

neologism that connotes in a deliberately confused manner homosexuals, pro-European intellectuals, and liberal politicians.

67. For more on the application of this doctrine, see M.A. Kışlalı, *Güneydogu: Düşük Yoğunlukta Çatışma* (Ankara: Ümit Yayıncılık, 1996).

68. The term "translator" refers to politically engaged intellectuals who, while condemning violence, try to understand the reasons behind it and establish a "dialogue" between the meanings embraced by the opposition and those meanings that are dominant. H. Böll and G. Grass played such a role in Germany of the 1960s and 1970s. See H.-J. Klein, *La mort mercenaire: Témoignage d'un ancien terroriste ouest-allemand* (Paris: Seuil, 1980).

69. According to repeated opinion polls, less than 15% of the electors still trust any one of the three governmental coalition parties in Turkey.

70. Ü. Cizre, *Muktedirlerin Siyaseti* (Istanbul: İletişim, 1999).

71. See among many others, R. Çakir, *Derin Hizbullah: İslamcı Şiddetin Geleceği* (Istanbul: Metis, 2001).

72. D. Ögüt, "Silahlanan Kirmizi Bölge," *Aydınlık,* 1–15 October, 1993.

73. "Silahi Kim Verirse Ona Hizmet Ederiz," *Hürriyet,* 17 December 1996.

74. For numerous examples of reinvention, see Erbil Tuşalp, *Bozkurtlar: Töreden Partiye* (Istanbul: Donkişot Yayınları, 2001).

75. The high military authorities recently expressed their solidarity with a military officer, Korkut Eken, who has been condemned for his involvement in the Susurluk scandal. As they declared, "he has done what he has done in conformity with the military chain of the command." See "Üç Paşadan Daha Destek: Emekli Orgeneral Doğu, Emekli Korgeneral Kurtaran ile Emekli Orgeneral Koman da Eken'e 'Yanındayız' Mesajı Verdi," *Hürriyet,* 14 February 2002.

76. In fact, the accident happened at a moment of high internal tension and struggle between the intelligence agencies. They brought the struggle between them into the public arena by engaging in a complex game of leaking secret documents and tape recordings concerning the activities of their adversary agencies.

77. However, for a general overview and some highly significant biographies, see Frank Bovenkerk and Yücel Yeşilgöz, *Türkiye'nin Mafyası* (Istanbul: İletişim, 2000).

78. İ. Ortaylı, *Osmanlı Toplumunda Aile* (Istanbul: Pan, 2000).

79. During the 1980s and 1990s, the geographic mobility of the youth and economic pauperization reinforced the category of the "street children,"

but a situation comparable to the Latin American cases has not emerged, not least because Turkey's street children invented their own internal mechanisms of regulation and, ultimately, recognized the authority of the "white-bears" (elders).

80. The "Abiler" (the big brothers) was the definition given to the oldest militants, whose ages fell in the range of eighteen to twenty-five.

81. Thirty-seven intellectuals, mainly of Alevi origin, died in a fire set during a riot provoked by thousands of radical right and Islamist militants.

82. The riots in the Gazi neighborhood in Istanbul started after the bombing of a coffee shop frequented by Alevi customers. Twenty-five Alevi militants were killed by the police during the riots.

83. Dev-Sol (Revolutionary Left, alias DHKP-C, Revolutionary Party-Front of People's Liberation) and TKP-ML (Communist Party of Turkey - Marxist-Leninist) were founded at the very beginning of the 1970s.

84. See *Kongre Belgeleri-2, DHKP Kuruluş Kongresi Kararları*, Istanbul, June, 1995.

85. One should, however, add that there are also many non-Alevi militants among them.

86. This operation showed that the imprisoned militants had no possibility of negotiating their conflict with the state. On the contrary, the state wanted to destroy their dignity as militants and as prisoners, and, in the case of failure, target their very existence.

87. S. Oruç, "Justice Ministry's Ertosun: 86 Prisoners Continue Death Fasts," *Turkish Daily News,* March 12, 2002. According to Ali Suat Ertosun, the head of the Prison Department of the Justice Ministry, out of the country's 57,681 prisoners, 8,243 persons were charged with being linked with terrorist organizations, and 1,067 with being members of criminal gangs.

88. M. Çayan, killed in 1972 by the security forces, was the founder of the THKP-C (Revolutionary Party-Front of People's Liberation). Dev-Sol, mentioned above, is an offspring of this organization.

89. For M. Çayan's text and comments on the text, see "Iyi Bak Bize Fasist Duvar. Iyi Tani Bizi... Seni Yerle Bir Edecek Olan Adalılar'ı İyi Tanı" in the semi-official organ of Dev-Sol, *Kurtuluş*, no. 43 (2000): 327–46.

90. As L. Martinez has shown, political struggle, economics, small-time criminality, and youth socialization processes all constitute

different facets of the single phenomenon of violence. See L. Martinez, *La guerre civile en Algerie: 1990–1998* (Paris: Karthala, 1998).

91. Alfred Morabia, *Le Gihad dans l'islam médieval* (Paris: Albin Michel, 1993).

92. Maxime Rodinson, *L'islam politique et croyance* (Paris: Fayard, 1994).

93. Bernard Lewis, *The Political Language of Islam* (Chicago: University of Chicago Press, 1988).

94. P. Larzillière, "Le phénomène du martyr dans les territoires palestiniens," paper presented to the IISMM colloquium, "Les sciences sociales à l'épreuve des événements d'Afghanistan," Paris, March 28–29, 2002; D. François, "Les brigades des martyrs d'Arafat," *Libération*, March 24, 2002.

95. Peter Blickle, ed., *Resistance, Representation and Community* (London: European Science Foundation, Clarendon Press, 1997).

96. Şerif Mardin, "Center-Periphery Relations: A Key to Turkish Politics," *Daedalus* 102, no. 1 (1973): 169–90.

97. A. K. S. Lambton, *Landlord and Peasant in Persia* (London: Oxford University Press, 1969, p. 291).

98. S. al Khalil (alias Kanan Makiya), *Republic of Fear* (Berkeley, Calif.: University of California Press, 1989); M. Seurat, *L'Etat de Barbarie* (Paris: Seuil, 1989).

99. As Omar Carlier suggests with regard to the Algerian case, this official unanimism combined two imperatives: *tawhid*, the Islamic imperative to recognize the fundamental unity of God, and the Jacobin imperative of "indivisibility." Omar Carlier, *Entre Nation et Djihad: Histoire sociale des radicalismes algériens* (Paris: Presses de Sciences Po, 1995), p. 248.

100. G. Denoeux, *Urban Unrest in the Middle East: A Comparative Study of Informal Networks in Egypt, Iran, and Lebanon* (Albany: State University of New York Press, 1993).

101. Henry Munson, *Islam and the Revolution in the Middle East* (New Haven, Conn.: Yale University Press, 1988).

102. M. De Certeau, *La culture au pluriel* (Paris: Seuil, 1993), p. 26.

103. Bernard Lewis, *The Political Language of Islam*; B. Sourati, "L'espace de la *dawla* dans le monde arabe musulman," *Maghreb Machrek*, no. 123 (1989): 71–79.

104. Michael Herb, *All in the Family: Absolutism, Revolution and Democracy in the Middle Eastern Monarchies* (Albany: State University of New York Press, 1999).

105. F. Georgeon, "La justice en plus: les Jeunes Turcs et la Révolution française," *ANKA*, no. 10 (1990): 21–32.

106. M.S. Hanioğlu, *Preparation for a Revolution: The Young Turks, 1902–1908* (New York: Oxford University Press, 2001); H. Bozarslan, "Vocabulaire politique de la violence: l'exemple jeune turc," in F. Georgeon and E. Copeaux, *Les mots du politique de l'Empire ottoman à la Turquie kémaliste, Documents de travail* (Paris: CHDT [EHESS], 1999), pp. 45–54.

107. Regarding the Kemalist Ministry of Justice Recep Peker wrote in the 1930s that "using the maximum of violence" was one of the characteristics of the Turkish Revolution." Recep Peker, *İnkılâp Ders Notları* (Istanbul: İletişim, 1984), p. 424.

108. Michel Aflaq, *Choix des textes de la pensée du fondateur du parti Ba'ath. Unité-Liberté-Socialisme* (Madrid: n.p., 1977), p. 88.

109. Kanan Makiya, *The Monument: Art, Vulgarity and Responsibility in Iraq* (Berkeley: University of California Press, 1991).

110. M. Hizal, T. Başoğlu, "Cumhuriyet Döneminde Heykelcilik," *Cumhuriyet Dönemi Türkiye Ansiklopedisi*, vol. 4 (Istanbul, İletişim, 1983), pp. 886–906.

111. B. Stora, "Algérie: absence et surabondance de mémoire," *Esprit*, no. 1 (1995): 67.

112. Daniel Pipes, *The Hidden Hand: Middle East Fears of Conspiracy* (New York: St. Martin's, 1996). Although extremely brief on Israel and Turkey, Pipes' work gives a broad overview of conspiracy theories in the Arab Middle East.

113. In a recent interview with the French newspaper *Le Monde*, the Israeli Interior Minister explained that the Palestinians would accept Israel's conditions only when they lose all hope, and only force could lead to such a result. *Le Monde*, December 14, 2001.

114. See, for example, Kanan Makiya, "The Arab World After September 11," *Dissent* (Spring 2002): 5–12.

115. G. Elwert, S. Feuchwang, and D. Neubert, eds., *Dynamics of Violence*.

116. For example, the circumstances of the 1980s and 1990s precluded the peaceful integration of the militants of Dev-Sol into Turkish politics, whereas many of those Islamists who renounced violence could maintain some small hope for eventual recognition.

160

117. N. Kermani, "Die Gärten der Märtyrer," *TAZ-Bericht*, November 20, 2001.

118. As experienced in Latin America, a movement initiated by a small revolutionary group to incite the masses to revolt against the establishment.

119. As Makiya puts it, "Atta and al-Jarrah lived through—on the ground, not in exile or in the West—the practical consequences of the failure of my generation's well-intentioned dreams and hopes. We, by and large, either sold out to our homegrown autocracies and tyrannies or packed our bags and left. . . . But the generation that followed ours mostly stayed behind; they had to fight the wars, and dodge the bullets, and therefore in an important sense, they had to pay the price for our failure, a price that we were unwilling to pay or fortunate enough not to have to pay." Makiya, "The Arab World after September 11."

120. Norman R. Cohn, *The Pursuit of the Millennium, Revolutionary Millenarians and Mystical Anarchists of the Middle Ages* (London: Paladin, 1984).

121. J.B. Rule, *Theories of Civil Violence*.